WHAT YOUR DOG IS THINKING

*The Science Behind Your Dog's Behaviour
and How to Improve It*

DR SABRINA COHEN-HATTON
and DANNY WELLS

T0385377

ROBINSON

ROBINSON

First published in Great Britain in 2025 by Robinson

Copyright © Sabrina Cohen-Hatton and Danny Wells, 2025

3 5 7 9 10 8 6 4

The moral rights of the authors have been asserted.

A CIP catalogue record for this book
is available from the British Library.

ISBN: 978-1-47214-903-9

Typeset in Bembo by Hewer Text UK Ltd, Edinburgh
Printed and bound in Great Britain by Clays Ltd, Elcograf S.p.A.

Papers used by Robinson are from well-managed forests and
other responsible sources.

Robinson
An imprint of
Little, Brown Book Group
Carmelite House
50 Victoria Embankment
London EC4Y 0DZ

The authorised representative
in the EEA is
Hachette Ireland
8 Castlecourt Centre
Dublin 15, D15 XTP3, Ireland
(email: info@hbgi.ie)

An Hachette UK Company
www.hachette.co.uk

www.littlebrown.co.uk

To all the dogs that are misunderstood –
and to all the owners who are trying to help them.

We see you.

Contents

Contents

Introduction

We've all had that one dog – the one that provides such inexpressible comfort that we crave their company. They're the dogs we miss when we go to work and the ones that make us want to normalise bringing dogs as a 'plus one'. That one dog we love so much that we find ourselves choking up at the thought that one day we might lose them. That one dog is our *soul dog*.

Our own soul dogs are the origin story of this book. We'll start with Danny's, a Belgian Malinois crossed with a German Shepherd, called Brodie. He was a stunning boy, with soft, black-and-tan graduated markings across his body, adding a sleekness to his muscular stature. His black muzzle swept around his mouth, making him look almost like that infamous supervillain, the Joker, and his upright ears pointed to the sky. Brodie was a formidable-looking dog, but he had another physical feature that made him special: his piercing, orange eyes. They were deeply kind, intelligent and soulful eyes. Looking into them was quite stirring. It was as if they were a window to an old soul, a soul that was profoundly intertwined with Danny's.

Trained by Danny as a champion protection dog, Brodie was utterly remarkable. He performed so well in working dog trials that he earned his place in the history books as one of Europe's top 100 Belgian Malinois. Danny and Brodie were inseparable, both on and off the trial fields.

Brodie was a challenging but extraordinarily capable dog. Danny's connection with him was so natural that it bordered on innate. That level of understanding enabled them to communicate in a way that made them unbeatable. Danny learned a lot from Brodie. In fact, the connection they had caused him to change his approach to training dogs completely.

Danny had learned from many excellent and experienced trainers during his years in the industry, but Brodie brought something different to the table. He didn't always respond in the way that the textbook said he should. Let's just say, he didn't always choose the treat over the squirrel!

Danny could tell Brodie was capable of much more, and he was inspired to experiment with different approaches to train him and to develop new techniques. But most importantly, Brodie taught Danny that every dog is an individual, with its own quirks and style – in the same way as every person is unique. Brodie pushed Danny away from the idea that all dogs learn in one certain way. Instead, dogs have different personalities, temperaments, motivations and genetics, all of which affect their behaviour. Danny now tailors his training to each unique dog in front of him.

Sadly, Brodie was taken too soon, when he was just four-and-a-half years old. Losing Brodie hit Danny like a freight train. The indescribable grief that he experienced sent him on a mission to give people and their dogs the best life they can have in the time they have together. Which, frankly, is far too short.

Brodie's legacy lives on in every dog Danny trains – and with many years of experience, that number runs into tens of thousands. With compassion, empathy and clear communication, he has helped many clients train their pet dogs to a standard of obedience like Brodie's. Most had thought their dogs were untrainable and were stunned at the results. Importantly for Danny, his style of training creates a stronger bond between dog and human, giving them new freedoms that they had previously assumed were beyond their reach. This doesn't necessarily require the same level of time and commitment that you would need to train a working dog, but the foundations result in exceptionally well-trained pet dogs. Every member of Danny's team of trainers has their own 'Brodie' – the one dog who's challenged them and helped them hone their expertise.

For some of us, that one dog, that soul dog, frustrates us beyond belief. We love them so much, but they behave in a way that challenges us, pushing us to our limits. But, as we know, some of the best things come out of adversity. Dr Sab's soul dog is one such dog. Luther is an incredibly handsome, dark, chiselled, *completely hairless* Mexican Xoloitzcuintle.

According to ancient Aztec mythology, the Xolo was created by Xolotl, the god of the Underworld, fire and lightning. Luther certainly wouldn't look out of place at the gates of hell, with his pointed upright ears, piercing eyes and leathery skin. He looks more like a demon than a *Canis lupus*. Despite his somewhat unusual looks, he is Dr Sab's favourite friend. Even if he does attract strange looks from passers-by.

Xolos are one of the few true, primitive breeds surviving today. Their wild tendencies are clear, having been moulded by evolution rather than selective breeding. They have a strong prey drive, triggering them to chase anything that moves, and they are anxious around strangers. They have an inbuilt survival mechanism that makes them innately wary of potential dangers.

Having owned Xolos previously, Dr Sab was well acquainted with all these foibles before she had Luther. She started training him as a puppy, then took him to obedience and agility clubs. He has always been like her shadow, going everywhere with her and sticking to her like Velcro. However, the qualities that make the Xolo so good at surviving in the wild made it harder for Luther to thrive amongst people. He just wanted to chase small, fluffy dogs, and new people made him anxious. So, although he was a model dog when he was on his own with Dr Sab, he needed a bit more help to understand that the world wasn't out to get him.

Luther led Dr Sab to Danny, who used the dog-centred approach he developed with Brodie to show Luther how to relax, which allowed them to take his obedience to the next level. Spending time with Danny at his Unleashed K9 training centre, Dr Sab saw dog after dog, believed to be irredeemable, completely changed by Danny and his team. Many of the dogs were aggressive towards people and other dogs. Most had already been to multiple trainers, none of whom could help them address their behavioural issues. Some had been deemed a lost cause, and behaviourists had already recommended euthanasia. Fortunately, their owners found Danny, their last hope for redemption. And it paid off. With care, understanding and a forensic knowledge of how dogs learn, Danny gave them a second chance.

Dr Sab was curious – not only in a dog-obsessed way, but also in a science-obsessed way. With a PhD in behavioural neuroscience, her research at Cardiff University focuses on how humans and animals learn and the factors that drive their decisions. She wanted to better understand how we can help more dogs with behavioural problems at their last-chance saloon, so she began a study. Danny, along with other trainers across the UK, started to help Dr Sab collect data to feed into the study, all working together towards improving the welfare of dogs.

Danny and Dr Sab share a curiosity about dogs' behaviour. Behind every behaviour witnessed there is a myriad of brain connections, neurobiological reactions and activity. Neurons fire and trigger other parts of the brain to light up, chemicals are released into the brain and body, and a thick soup of emotions underlies it all. If you think of the dog's brain as a supercomputer, millions of calculations underpin each output, which we then see as a behaviour.

Dogs have done incredibly well at living with people for tens of thousands of years. The science shows that they've evolved the most spectacular brain mechanisms that draw them closer to people, which hasn't been seen in any other species. Unlike other animals, parts of their brains are dedicated to reading emotion in human voices, and other parts are super-sensitive to human faces. Their genes predispose them to bond with people, and their neurobiological systems have evolved to experience 'love' similarly to humans. When they cuddle with their owner, they release oxytocin – the love hormone – just as people do with each other. There's a reason dogs are our best friends: their brains are hardwired for that relationship.

Yet dogs have it tough. Despite being in loving homes, with all their creature comforts, they're seldom understood. You see, we love them so much that we too readily treat them like four-legged people. We mistake their intentions for human intentions. We judge their behaviour as we would human behaviour. And so we're sometimes unfair to them, thinking they're deliberately ignoring us when they simply don't understand in the way we think they do. By assuming human qualities – or anthropomorphising – not only do we sometimes miss what they actually need, but we also so easily miss out on their inherent beauty as dogs.

Danny and Dr Sab want to use everything they've learned from both science and practical dog training to help you understand what your dog is thinking and why those thoughts result in unhelpful behaviours at times. Like going crazy at the doorbell, ignoring you as you call them back over the park, or ripping the bin bag open as soon as our backs are turned (and looking particularly guilty about it).

In the following pages, we will take a deep dive into the science behind dogs' thoughts and behaviour. We will use cutting-edge research to unpack common myths about dogs and their relationships with people.

Each chapter focuses on common behavioural problems and takes you on a walk through the 'science park' to show what's happening in your dog's brain at the time. We have carefully chosen stories about dogs and their owners* to bring the studies to life using anecdotes

---

* We have changed the names of all the dogs, their owners' names and descriptions to preserve anonymity.

everyone with a dog will recognise. All the stories are based on the tens of thousands of dogs Danny has helped over the years. At the end of each chapter, we will guide you through science-backed exercises you can practise at home with your own dog.

There are lots of things you can try to improve your dog's behaviour. Some of the exercises will teach you how to do new things with your dog, like sniffing out your keys. Others address common behavioural problems, such as barking at the doorbell or pulling on the lead. Feel free to mix and match when teaching any new things, but note that if you're working on specific problem behaviours these might need a little more attention. We would recommend tackling these one at a time, so you can make sure they're dealt with before you move on.

We hope that this book will help you learn more about the inner world of your dog so that you can apply that greater understanding to your everyday interactions. We hope it helps you strengthen your bond with your dog even more. Who knows – maybe you'll even get another ... or seven! But however many dogs share your life and home with you, we're certain you'll have a better relationship with them after reading this book.

Chapter 1

What your dog is thinking about you

'Other' might strike you as an unusual name for a dog. However, Other was quite an unusual dog. An odd combination of a Vizsla crossed with a Shar Pei, he was about the size of a small Labrador. He had a short, ginger coat that felt like velvet. Other looked as if his skin was just a little too big for him – a bit like his attitude to life.

Despite being an incredibly loving and affectionate dog, he had absolutely zero spatial awareness. He would wiggle through the house with his tail swooshing so hard it knocked over anything in his path. And anything that survived his tail would likely get bumped out of the way by his jiggly bum. Nothing was safe from his clumsiness, and he wasn't the slightest bit bothered. Convinced that the entire world existed solely for his benefit, he gave off the sense that life was his movie – and that he was the star.

Anita and Toby, a young couple, adopted Other a couple of years ago. Anita was desperate for a dog. For months, she had spent her lunchtime at the investment bank where she worked scrolling through her phone and looking at profiles of dogs needing a home. Toby was less enthusiastic. He was a freelance graphic designer, so he often worked from home and had little desire to add another chore to his day while Anita was out at work.

Eventually, worn down by Anita's relentless enthusiasm, Toby relented and agreed that they would get a dog. They found Other through a friend of a friend who had an accidental litter of puppies after their neighbour's Shar Pei chewed a hole in the fence with less than honourable intentions for visiting their Vizsla, who was on heat. At six months old, Other was the last of the litter to find a home. But as soon as Anita saw him, she knew he would be perfect. He wobbled up to them in the living room of his puppyhood home, ginger wrinkles drowning his face and paws so big they looked like they should be his dad's. He plonked himself down in front of Anita and Toby and lay on his back with his tail wagging, baring his pink belly and inviting them to scratch it.

'He's perfect,' squealed Anita.

Toby shrugged.

'I guess he's coming home with us then.'

Anita knew that it was going to work out. She had everything planned. She would walk the pup morning and night, she would train him to do tricks – she'd already found some great videos on YouTube – and she would teach herself everything she needed to know so that Toby wouldn't be proved right in his assumption that he'd be the one left to do everything. Plus, he was already well on his way to being house-trained (Other, not Toby), so that was one less thing she would have to figure out.

You might be wondering how Other got his name. When they arrived home on Other's 'gotcha day', Anita could sense that Toby didn't share her excitement. She'd wanted a dog for so long and was desperate for it to work. She wanted him to love the dog as much as she did, so she had an idea that she hoped would make him more invested.

'I think you should name him,' Anita said, stroking the dog's ear softly as he sat between her and Toby on the sofa.

'Really?' replied Toby. He was surprised, but touched by Anita's sincerity. 'I mean, I would, but I really wouldn't have the first clue what to call him.'

'Don't worry, I'll send you a couple of options, and you can mull them over.'

Anita pulled up her phone, and after a few minutes of pretend searching for dog names, she opened WhatsApp and typed her pre-prepared shortlist into a poll. 'Dirk', 'Doug', 'Derek' or 'other', just to ensure Toby had space to add his own name if he wanted (knowing very well that he wouldn't). She had always wanted a dog with a human name. Feeling quite pleased with herself, she had combined the grand gesture of letting Toby name the dog while remaining safe in the knowledge it would be one of the names she wanted. She smiled to herself smugly and sent the message to Toby.

Almost immediately, her phone pinged with a response.

' "Other",' it read. Anita furrowed her brow and responded.

'You can't just say "Other". You need to suggest something. That's how a poll works when it gives you the option for "other".'

'Then I chose "Other" ... I think it's a great name for a dog,' he replied.

'You can't be serious?'

'You said I could choose. I chose "Other".'

Anita sighed. Other looked up at Anita, and she was sure he rolled his eyes. Either way, he was named.

Despite Anita's enormous love for Other, she was convinced he preferred Toby to her. Whenever she and Toby arrived home together, as soon as the front door opened, Other would rush towards them excitedly. His tail would wag so furiously that his haunches would wiggle hard from side to side and his toes would patter across the black-and-white Victorian floor tiles. When Anita outstretched her arms to greet him with 'Hello boy!', he would give her a cursory sniff before showering Toby with affection. He would nuzzle and flop his body onto Toby's legs as he gazed up at his face, tongue flopping goof-ily out of the side of his mouth and tail wagging even harder. Anita would call him over, and he would glance at her briefly before return-ing to Toby to collect extra scritches. It was infuriating for Anita. After all, Toby hadn't even wanted the dog. It was her idea. She didn't want to be jealous, but she couldn't help but feel it gripping the pit of her stomach.

She became convinced that Other preferred Toby to her. When she and Toby sat on the sofa together, relaxing in the evening, Other would lie with his stout, orange head across Toby's lap, not hers. He would sometimes raise his head to lick Toby's face, while Toby chuckled and sang his rendition of 'Mr Other, Other . . .' Shaggy style. Anita would sometimes get kisses, but with nowhere near as much enthusiasm. Other would nap on Toby's side of the bed when she was at work. Anita hoped this was because she usually left their soft, fleecy throw strewn on his side, but deep down she knew it was because it smelled of Toby. And when they walked Other together, the dog would ignore Anita's attempts at recalling him but would listen to Toby instantly. 'You Otherfucker,' Anita would murmur to herself.

Anita found it all so frustrating. After all, she and Toby both lived with Other. They both took turns to feed him, both walked him, and both loved him equally. So, what is it that makes you important to your dog? What is it that some people do that makes dogs like them over other people?

Researchers from the University of Vienna and the brilliantly named Clever Dog Lab Society set out to investigate how dogs' relationship with people influences their attention.[1] They wanted to see what part of the dog–human relationship affected a dog's focus. They weren't convinced that it was just a case of the dog knowing someone. Rather, they wanted to explore whether there could be something about their specific relationship that determines where the dog directs its attention. This point is especially relevant for dogs like Other, who live with and interact with more than one person but seem to have developed a closer bond with one of them.

The study took twenty-four dogs living with two people in the same household. The researchers divided the dogs into two groups, based on the level of interaction and care they had from each person.

In one group, both people were equally as engaged with their dog's care; in the other group, only one person in the house really bothered. The idea behind the study was that in a house with two people, those who interact more with the dog would have a closer relationship. They wanted to see if this closeness – rather than just familiarity – made any difference to the way dogs would focus their attention.

The researchers set up three boxes in a quiet room and brought in three people: the two people the dog lived with, and a stranger. Each person had to interact with the boxes in various ways designed to elicit the dog's attention to a greater or a lesser degree. For example, they had to crouch down with the box, touch it or search inside it noisily. The experimenters told them not to call for the dog's attention; they wanted to see which person the dog was naturally most drawn to.

The results showed that dogs paid much more attention to the people who interacted most with them. In fact, in homes where one person didn't bother much, the dogs only gave them about the same amount of attention as they did to a stranger.

Familiarity with a dog alone wasn't sufficient to warrant their attention. Rather, the quality of the relationship was by far the most critical factor. People who spent time interacting with their dogs seemed to forge a better bond with them, and their dogs were more interested in them. It's similar to any friendship group: you might like everyone in it, but there may be one person you get on with best, spend the most time with or would be the first person you call when you've got a problem. It's the same with dogs.

It wasn't that Other didn't like Anita: he did. But he forged a much closer relationship with Toby. Part of the reason was because Toby worked at home, so he found himself doing more activities with Other. He would sit at his computer with the dog resting his head in his lap, feeding him bits of digestive biscuit as he dunked them in his tea. At lunchtime, Toby would walk Other down to the local deli to pick up a toasted sandwich and a coffee. On their way back, they would stop at the green and sit together while Toby ate his lunch. Then, they would round off with a quick game of fetch before heading back for the onslaught of afternoon emails. Although both Anita and Toby walked and fed Other, Toby interacted with him far more. He became the bringer of good things in Other's eyes, and so Other's eyes were naturally drawn to him more than to Anita.

It wasn't as simple as the amount of time they spent with each other; the quality of interaction they had during that time counted more. When Anita was at home, she pretty much just co-existed with Other. When she took him out for a walk, she usually had the lead in one hand and her phone in the other, trying to catch up with the day's social media. She loved Other greatly, but even though she was there, she was never really present. As the research shows, a strong relationship with your dog requires more than just giving it the bare essentials. It is *how* you interact with your dog that makes the most difference to your bond.

Given dogs have evolved alongside humans for tens of thousands of years, it's of little surprise that there is something special about their relationship with us. Research has found dogs are exquisitely sensitive to human social cues.[2] For example, they follow human gestures, such as pointing to find hidden food. This might sound simple, but humans can only do this well by about fourteen months of age, and chimpanzees struggle to do it at all. But dogs are more willing to follow social cues from humans. Even more incredibly, there seems to be an inherited element to this that has developed as dogs have evolved during domestication with people.

When a dog bonds with us, it feels pretty special. There is something deeply soothing about spending time in the company of your dog. We know from research that it doesn't just feel good; it positively affects our physiology. The amount of cortisol – the stress hormone – reduces, and our blood pressure decreases.[3] For Toby, the mere sight of Other made him feel good. It wasn't something he could define precisely, just that warm fuzzy feeling when you're around another being you enjoy spending time with. You have good experiences with them. But how does it feel for your dog? How can we find out what value they truly put on their relationship with us?

Neuroscientists at Emory University in Atlanta, Georgia, have given us a glimpse into the inner workings of the canine brain that might help us to answer that question.[4] They used functional magnetic resonance imaging – fMRI for short – which is a technology that maps a person's brain activity on a screen as their thoughts unfold. A group of scientists have pioneered this with dogs. While this process might not tell us exactly what our dogs are thinking, it certainly gives us a better insight as to what's happening in their brains.

An fMRI scanner is a huge, doughnut-shaped magnet so powerful that it's around thirty thousand times stronger than the Earth's magnetic field. When people – or in this case, dogs – are scanned, the magnetic field interacts with hydrogen atoms inside the body, aligning them in a particular direction. Different regions of the brain need more oxygen as the brain engages in various tasks or responds to stimuli that the experimenters present. Blood increases in these active areas, and fMRI detects these changes. It's a bit like a real-time movie of your brain at work.

As good as the technology is, it has limitations. Brain scanning in this way measures blood flow, not neural activity, i.e. which neurons activate during a mental function. It's like trying to judge a car's speed by looking at the exhaust fumes. You get a good indication, but not the whole picture. It requires a degree of 'guestimation'.

The complexity of the brain also needs to be considered. The brain is more than just a collection of distinct and isolated regions responsible for specific tasks: it's a highly interconnected network. Different parts of the brain collaborate to produce thoughts, emotions and actions. So when you see a specific area 'light up' on a brain scan, it isn't as simple as saying that part of the brain is responsible solely for a particular function. It's much more of a team effort, and fMRI only gives us the highlight reel. Then there is the issue of 'noise'. Subjects need to stay still inside the scanner, which can be easier said than done. Small movements of the head, even breathing, can result in fluctuations that skew the data. It's like getting a fuzzy picture when someone moves in the middle of a shot. Researchers use complex algorithms to filter out the noise, but it's an ongoing challenge.

These difficulties aside, the technology gives us valuable insights into what might happen in our dogs' brains. This study hoped to find out exactly how much people mean to their dogs through their strongest sense, *olfaction* – their sense of smell. It looked at what happened in the brain when dogs were exposed to various scents. They were particularly interested in the *caudate nucleus*, a region of the brain involved in processing positive expectations and rewards. The researchers wanted to see what was happening in the dog's brain when it smelled a human or a dog they knew and then compare it to what happened when they smelled one they didn't know, to see if the relationship triggered something different.

A group of twelve dogs were trained to stay still inside an fMRI scanner and were presented with various smells. Scents were collected from the armpits of humans using a sterile gauze pad, and from the 'business end' of dogs (in other words, their privates). The scents included the dog itself, a familiar human, a stranger, a familiar dog and an unfamiliar dog.

The scans revealed that the scent of a familiar human activated the caudate nucleus – the pleasure centre – the most. This finding was significant as it showed that dogs not only differentiated that scent from others – so they definitely recognised their humans – but also had a distinct positive emotional response to them: even more so than when they recognised the scent of a familiar dog.

It's a bit like when you smell the perfume or aftershave of your favourite person, or the smell of cinnamon buns 'like your gran used to make'. It whisks you back to her kitchen in a wave of nostalgia. That emotional response – that warm fuzzy feeling – is likely down to your caudate nucleus. It's a critical part of the brain's reward system. It receives signals from the prefrontal cortex, which is responsible for functions like decision-making and planning, and from the *amygdala*, a major processing centre for emotions. It also has links to the hippocampus, which processes memory. These inputs help the caudate nucleus evaluate the potential reward that something signals, based on how the dog is feeling at that time, as well as on past experiences.

Based on these evaluations, the caudate nucleus sends signals to other parts of the brain to drive the dog's behaviour. For instance, it's part of a system[*] that connects to dopamine-producing regions of the brain.[†] When you experience something rewarding, the release of dopamine feels good, reinforcing the behaviour that led to the reward. The more often this circuit is triggered, the more your dog will anticipate good things from you.

The findings from this study show that dogs' strong positive association with their humans is seriously gratifying to them. There is something special about this relationship: even something that triggers the memory of a person that a dog has bonded with makes it feel really good. The smell of its person activates the caudate nucleus, creating an anticipation of a sense of pleasure and happiness. It's like

---

[*] If you're interested in the geeky bits, this part of the brain is called the *striatum*, which includes the *putamen* and the nucleus accumbens.
[†] Like the *Ventral Tegmental Area* (VTA).

smelling our favourite comfort food on a cold and rainy day and feeling instantly soothed. Not because you're eating the food, but because the idea of the food feels good. In the case of a dog, it's entirely plausible that this kind of relationship serves as an emotional anchor, making it feel secure. This might be why Other liked to sleep on Toby's side of the bed; it felt comforting, like the smell on a pillow of someone you miss.

On the face of it, it seems very much as if the connection between dog and person is driven by some sense of mutual love and trust. But is the human the critical part – or is it what the human represents? We feed our dogs and dispense treats willingly. So, is it simply that our dogs feel good when they see this because they associate us with food, and it's the idea of food that's making them feel good – not the thought of us?

Another study might help us to answer this question. A team of neuroscientists, Peter Cook, Ashley Prichard, Mark Spivak and Gregory Berns, set up an experiment to understand whether dogs preferred food rewards or social interaction with a person.[5] Entitled 'Awake canine fMRI predicts dogs' preference for praise vs food', it used brain scanning again to help understand the biological underpinnings of the relationship between dogs and people and how this can vary from dog to dog.

Dogs were trained to associate three different objects (that were new to them) with three different outcomes. A toy car, a toy horse and a hairbrush were each paired with food, verbal praise and nothing. For instance, every time a toy car was held up in front of the dog, food would follow. A hairbrush would be followed by praise, and a toy horse would be followed with nothing at all. The dog would quickly begin to know that the toy predicted whatever followed it. Once the dogs understood this concept, they were put in a brain scanner and presented with the three objects to see what activity would be triggered in the brain. Again, the scientists were particularly interested in the brain's reward centre, a specific part of the caudate nucleus called the *ventral caudate*. The caudate nucleus, as a whole, is involved in a broad range of functions, and the ventral caudate is the part that is most involved with the brain's reward system.[6]

The study found that the ventral caudate was much more active when the dogs were presented with an item that signalled praise or food than with the object that signalled nothing. So, the researchers were undoubtedly looking in the right place in the brain. Interestingly, almost 87 per cent of dogs had equal or more activation for praise than for food. In a follow-on experiment outside the scanner, dogs were presented with the two items that could get them praise or food and were allowed to choose between them by approaching the items. And guess what? Their choices correlated strongly with their brain activity in the scanner. Those with greater activation in the ventral caudate when expecting praise chose praise over food, and vice versa. Dogs with similar activity didn't show much of a preference between praise or food. This shows how dogs are individuals with their own distinct preferences. Part of the joy of having a new dog is working out what it likes and what its quirks are. Just like any new relationship.

What we can see from this study is that the pleasure dogs get from interacting with us means more to them than just food (which is quite incredible when you consider how inherently vital food is to dogs). For many dogs, praise alone is a powerful reinforcer of behaviour. When training Other, Toby usually found that praise was the best way to reward him for doing something right once he had learned a command, like sitting or staying. And it was much better for his diet than constantly feeding him extra treats. More importantly, using praise to reinforce behaviours further strengthened their mutual bond and helped provide Other with clarity about what Toby wanted. It was a communication tool as much as a bonding tool.

We perhaps shouldn't be surprised by this, given that humans are a part of the social groups that dogs have lived in for thousands of years.

Arguably, evolution has shaped their brains to be sensitive to human cues and actions. So, our relationship with dogs is relevant at a profound, biological level. The connection isn't just behavioural – it's neurobiological.

One useful physiological indicator of this is a neurotransmitter called *phenylethylamine*. A neurotransmitter is a chemical messenger that carries signals from one neuron to another, allowing impulses to pass from one cell to the next. Phenylethylamine is believed to be involved in attraction – the start of positive interactions.[7] It has an amphetamine-like effect, triggering feelings of elation and exhilaration. One study measured phenylethylamine to indicate how positive interactions were for humans and dogs, and to see if it was implicated at a cellular level,[8] and therefore could be involved in the ensuing behaviours.

Professor Johannes Odendaal of the Life Sciences Research Institute in Pretoria in South Africa, and his collaborator Dr Susan Lehmann, a biochemist at the Canadian Centre for Human and Animal Molecular Health in Winnipeg, Manitoba, divided eighteen humans and eighteen dogs into two groups. One group of humans interacted with their own dogs, and the other with unfamiliar dogs. The interactions took place in a quiet, neutral room and involved the humans talking softly to the dogs and stroking them. Both humans' and dogs' blood pressure were measured throughout. Blood pressure is often used as a physiological measure to gauge how stressed or relaxed someone is. If the interaction was relaxing, you would imagine blood pressure would reduce; if it was arousing, then it would increase. Blood samples were collected at various points to measure any changes in plasma levels of *phenylacetic acid*, a catabolite – or a product of the breaking down – of phenylethylamine.

The results showed that both humans and dogs experienced increased phenylacetic acid after a positive interaction. The increase persisted whether the humans and dogs were familiar with each other or not, suggesting that both found the interactions inherently positive. There was an interesting effect on blood pressure. It reduced significantly in people when interacting with their own dogs, but less so when interacting with unfamiliar dogs. On the other hand, dogs had reduced blood pressure when interacting with unfamiliar humans – suggesting they found that more relaxing. But there wasn't a significant decrease when interacting with their owners. That could be because they were more excited to see their owners. As a side note, the unfamiliar dogs were all used to being handled by many different people in various environments, so it's likely they were less excited by the situation.

Another study reinforced this by looking at a hormone called *oxytocin*,[9] which is involved in prosocial behaviours like forming bonds with others and keeping those bonds close.[10] The study took fifty-five volunteers and their dogs, and found that gazing into each other's eyes resulted in the release of oxytocin. Longer gazes produced more oxytocin, which suggests there is something about the interaction between dogs and people that is driving their attachment at a biological level.

What was clear from both studies was that dogs and people certainly experienced similar physiological responses to interacting with each other, which seemed to indicate the experience was a positive one. It seems that the bond between humans and dogs isn't just an emotional one, but a biochemical one too. It's perhaps no surprise then that the relationship is so strong. What's incredible is that these changes are happening across two different species.

Be present – don't just be there

We have seen from science that building a strong, social relationship with your dog means much more than just being around your dog. Instead, you need to be present. *Really* present. Not just in physical proximity, but mentally as well. Do you know that sense of happiness and anticipation when someone hands you a gift to unwrap? That's the positive anticipation you can strive to create between you and your dog, where you become the most valuable thing in their world, regardless of any other distractions.

Try this: Make your dog's name mean something
The name you choose for your dog might be meaningful to you, but how do you make it meaningful to your dog? The simple answer is that what you link it with will become a signal to your dog that allows it to predict what comes next, which over time will result in it paying attention when you call it.

The idea is to condition your dog to respond instantly to its name. When the dog hears it, a hit in its brain's pleasure centre should be imminent. To do this is relatively simple. Stand in front of your dog and say its name, make sure it's looking at you, and immediately follow with a treat. Whenever you want to teach your dog to do something new, use something it finds rewarding to encourage it to do it again. After doing this a few times, you can progress by waiting for your dog to look away, and calling its name again, rewarding it as soon as it looks at you.

Repeat this until you say your dog's name and it turns and looks at you consistently. It's a good idea to get in the habit of repeating the exercise a couple of times a day for the next few weeks, as you're going about your business. It doesn't need to be dedicated training time; just do it as and when you get the chance, to help build up an association between the name and getting something good.

Once your dog knows its name, it's time to build on that foundation so that it will respond to you whenever it hears it.

Say the name, and practise bringing different levels of joy when it looks at you. Sometimes, give your dog a bit of food. Other times, a simple 'good' and verbal praise. You could drop to your knees and fuss your dog physically while you praise it. Given what we know about the science, it would be worth taking note of the kind of reward your dog has a preference for. Not that this should become its sole reward; a bit of variety is the spice of good dog training.

Eventually, you can progress this to challenging your dog with something that's mildly distracting, but enough that might compete for their attention. Like holding a dog biscuit and drawing the dog's attention away from you, and then saying its name and rewarding it with a better treat (like cheese or meat – steak is always better than biscuits to a dog!) so it learns that giving attention to you is always worthwhile.

Through this exercise, the dog learns that not only does hearing its name lead to good things, but also that all those good things come from you. You are constantly strengthening your bond while ensuring your dog is always attentive to its name. Remember, this also means it'll be focused on you. You never know when that might be a lifesaver, enabling you to get your dog's attention before it notices something that will get it into trouble – like a tasty snack dropped on the floor that might be bad for it. Throw this exercise in freely whenever you're with your dog.

Try this: Make sure everything of value in some way involves you
Make yourself the primary source of fun for your dog. This doesn't mean incessantly showering your dog with treats, toys and fuss. While there's a place for that, what we mean here is ensuring that you are an intrinsic part of everything that your dog does. Make the time you spend with your dog count. When

you're walking, be present. Avoid scrolling on your phone or sending messages while you've got the lead in your hand. Make the most of your time together.

If you have toys for your dog, don't leave them out so that it can play with them when it feels like it. Instead, you bring out the toy and play with your dog. Whether it's a tug toy you can bring to life by holding on one end while your dog pulls the other, or a ball you can throw to play fetch with, make toys a symbol of playtime with you rather than something to distract your dog from you.

Try this: Teach your dog to relax
Teaching your dog to switch off and relax might be one of the most powerful ways to strengthen your bond. This might sound counterintuitive, but it's imperative for your dog to be contented when it is either with you in the face of distractions, or at home without you. Some dogs are fine with being home alone, while others struggle a little more. Some others experience separation anxiety. They become hypervigilant and experience negative emotions, resulting in unwanted behaviours, from nuisance barking to chewing up furniture, and in extreme cases they can even self-harm. This is one of the most common behavioural problems that owners report, and it can affect their bond with their dog. It can even reduce a dog's lifespan.[11]

The good news is that almost all dogs can benefit from steps you can take to reduce the anxiety they might experience when you're not around. The basis of this is a solid and healthy relationship with you – the emphasis being on healthy – where you can use routine to teach your dog what will happen daily, enabling it to predict outcomes. Dogs are always happier when they can predict the outcomes of a situation. It gives them a sense of familiarity and confidence because they know what will happen next.

The first step in teaching your dog to switch off is practising this at home. Here, you can control things that your dog might find distracting and, consequently, you can set it up for success.

Give your dog a safe space at home where it can relax and isn't free to roam around and practise behaviours you don't want – like scratching your doors or chewing your chair legs. A dog crate is an excellent option.

Dogs love dens – wild dogs will often use dens – and, when done right, a crate can provide your dog with the same sense of comfort and security. There are added benefits to getting your dog comfortable in a crate. If it is sick and needs to stay at the vet, it will likely spend some time in a crate. It will probably be in a crate if it needs to travel. So, whether you choose to use a crate as a regular fixture at home or have a free-roaming dog, it still pays to get your dog comfortable spending time in a den-like crate.

Make sure it is cosy, and put a dog bed or blankets inside so your dog has a comfy place to lie. It should also be large enough for your dog to stand up, turn around and stretch out. Ideally, place the crate in a room that you don't sleep in, so your dog gets comfortable with having time on its own. Most people use the kitchen or dining room, but it can be any room that suits. It's better to be somewhere that people aren't congregating (to begin with at least; we can change this later when your dog has got the hang of things), so your dog doesn't get over-stimulated when you're trying to teach it to switch off.

There is a lot of misinformation around crate training – and it's actually much easier than you might think. The crate should be somewhere your dog enjoys spending time. It's not to be used as a 'sin bin'. Instead, your dog should have good associations with spending time there. In most cases, you can create these good feelings by getting your dog to have good experiences in the crate. For example, put its food and water in there so that it associates the essentials it needs with being in the crate. A treat or two every time you put your dog in the crate can work as a positive precursor. If you're going to give your dog a dental chew, do so in the crate (make sure you vary the times so that the dog doesn't start to predict it and play up when the treat doesn't come, which might hinder its settling down).

You might find your dog barking or whining a little when you first start using a crate. This is normal; ignore it and let it settle down alone. Don't make a molehill into a mountain! The crate isn't generally a big issue, but overcomplicating it can lead to problems. If you respond to your dog's barks, it will quickly learn that barking brings you back, and will continue to bark to get you to return. If, however, your dog doesn't settle and shows signs of greater anxiety or behaviours that could be signs of distress, like chewing at the bars or destroying the bedding, stop and work with a trainer. Most dogs will settle relatively quickly, but some may need a little more work or an alternative approach.

Start practising this exercise when you have a few hours at home with your dog. Start small by popping your dog in the crate for short periods, just five or ten minutes before returning (but only when the dog is quiet), taking it out, and doing something with it.* This might be going for a walk, doing a little training, or playing a game of tug or fetch. The idea is that quiet time in the crate is followed by fun time with you, which is the

---

* This exercise assumes your dog is already familiar with the crate and is comfortable spending time in there. For dogs with existing behavioural problems or that already display high levels of separation anxiety, work with a reputable trainer to ensure the dog's behavioural issues are taken into consideration in a training plan.

foundation of your solid bond. It also teaches your dog that you always return. The more your dog experiences you returning, the more confident it will be that you always will and the less likely it will be to experience separation anxiety. At night, don't be afraid to pop your dog in the crate to sleep; they might whine a little, but should settle soon enough.

Once your dog is happy to spend time alone in the crate quietly, while you're pottering around at home, you can move on to teaching your dog to switch off in the house when it's out of the crate. Again, the key is to start small and build up. Patience is key!

Pop a 'house lead' on your dog – usually, a thinner, lighter version – that it can wear in the house. You don't need to hold it all the time. Your dog can go about its business with the lead trailing behind it. But having the lead there means you can grab hold of it and control your dog, to help it understand what you're asking it to do.

Choose a time when you're relaxing, like watching the TV or flicking through the papers, and have your dog sit or lie down next to your feet. If the dog tries to get up and move away, calmly use the lead to return it to its position by you, and carry on. Stay composed, without fussing or interacting too much. The idea should be that your dog is learning to relax, so getting it excited will set it up to fail. Be mindful not to do something that 'rewards' your dog for moving out of position, or 'breaking the stay', like giving it fuss or attention. This will tell it that moving out of position is fine and a surefire way of getting some rewarding interaction with you. Be boring – the fun comes later! One indicator that the dog is relaxed is an audible sigh, and it curls up. When you get that, you've nailed it.

Once your dog is happy to switch off in the house, try to take this up a level and teach it to relax with you when it's out

WHAT YOUR DOG IS THINKING

and about. Find a bench to sit on for a while, and sit your dog by your feet. There will be many more interesting things that compete for your dog's attention outside, be that other people walking by, sounds carried on the wind or interesting smells. It might feel like you're going back to basics, but be consistent and patient. When your dog looks at you, you can say 'good' and reward it. This reinforces that, in the face of distractions, focusing on you brings good things. If your dog gets up, put it back in position. With some consistency, your dog will soon be happy to sit with you calmly as the world goes by.

Then you can repeat the process in cafés, pubs and anywhere else you like to frequent with your dog. Remember: just as we are individuals, so are dogs. Some might settle quickly, and some might take more time. Always work with your dog and its specific needs. If your dog settles in the crate immediately, you might find you can progress through the stages more quickly. Others might take several weeks to learn to turn off in a particular place. Ensure your dog has reached that place of comfortably switching off before progressing to more distracting environments. Patience is key – you're in this for the long haul so don't be disheartened if it hasn't worked after a few days. You must be consistent.

These exercises will help build a strong relationship with your dog because they focus on socially interacting with you. Your dog does something with you and gets rewarded for the choices that involve paying attention to you. Paying attention to you becomes valuable. Before you know it, the mere sight of you is firing up your dog's caudate nucleus, and you become an effigy of happiness and joy. Now, if only we could have the same effect on our significant others!

Summary
- The quality of your relationship with your dog is more important than the quantity of time you spend with it.
- Make its name mean something by pairing it with a reward from you.
- Make the time you spend with your dog count. Interact with your dog and ensure everything of value involves you.
- Avoid leaving toys out for your dog and make playtime meaningful by being actively involved.
- Teach your dog how to relax when you're not around, by teaching it you'll always return.
- Teach your dog how to relax with you, seeing you as a source of trusted comfort, preferring your company to any of the distractions around it.

Chapter 2

What your dog is thinking
when you call it back

Dirk put his hand up to shade his eyes from the brightness of the early morning sun. He craned his neck towards the spot where his dog, Mollie Mischief, was rummaging in the distant bushes. He couldn't see her. Her location was only betrayed by the rustling nettles she was searching through, probably for the prize of an old, mouldy tennis ball or – even worse – some fox droppings to roll in and which he would have to scrape off before they stopped in the pub for lunch.

Dirk loved watching Mollie run around, just being a dog, particularly on a mild spring morning like today. He could feel the warmth of the sunshine on his cheek, reminding him of the comforting feeling he had inside when he thought about little Mollie and how much he enjoyed having her around.

Dirk was a tall, slender man with mousey brown hair and sunken grey eyes. He had a somewhat hollow face with cheekbones so pronounced his entire body seemed to hang from them. He was a widower, having lost his wife, Marcey, suddenly to an aggressive form of leukaemia.

Marcey was the love of his life, and it had hit him hard. For a while, Dirk felt utterly lost. He would do anything to try to feel close to her again. He'd wrap her old, comfy cardigan around his pillow to help him get to sleep, despite the annoying heart-shaped buttons that always seemed to work their way around to wherever he tried to rest his head. He continued to buy her favourite lemon and ginger herbal tea, despite hating both lemon and ginger. He would make himself a cup every morning and couldn't stomach more than two sips. But the smell of it was comfortingly familiar.

Marcey loved dogs. She would point out every dog she saw and announce their breed with startling accuracy, even the mixed breeds. She had wanted a dog, but at the time they were living in a small, rented flat in Balham, and their landlord wouldn't allow it. By the time they bought their own place in Clapham, Marcey fell ill, and their main focus was on her health.

In an attempt to ditch the repulsive tea and feel closer to his late wife, Dirk decided he would fulfil her wish posthumously and get himself a dog. A careful and considered man, he thought long and hard about it, weighing up his capacity to care for a dog with the work he expected he would have to put into its care. And although his deliberations took a long time, the decision to choose Mollie was more impulsive. He saw an advert on Facebook for a young dog in need of a home after her owner passed away.

The dog which appeared on his screen was a little black Staffordshire Bull Terrier with a white patch on her chest shaped like a heart, just like the buttons on his wife's old cardigan. Her ears were like cheese sandwich triangles curled on the top corner – remarkably similar to the ones Marcey used to pop in his lunch box for work. The Staffie's eyes were a rich mahogany brown and she always appeared to be smiling. Dirk thought his mind must be playing tricks. He had never seen a smiling dog before.

'It must be AI,' he muttered to himself. He leant forward at the screen and removed his glasses, squinting to take a closer look. He realised it was, in fact, a smiling, bereaved dog with a chest marking that reminded him of Marcey's buttons.

The parallels were uncanny; he clicked the link and wrote a message. He had a reply almost instantaneously and went to pick up little Mollie Mischief that afternoon. She had already been named

Mollie, but he added the 'Mischief' when she stole a bite of his Rich Tea biscuit right after he dunked it in his tea (he'd given up the dreadful herbal stuff at last).

In his grief, he hadn't thought he would ever allow himself the pleasure of feeling joy again. So, these little moments with Mollie meant a great deal to Dirk. Mollie Mischief was as giddy as they come, and he loved watching her dart around the playing fields on such a lovely morning. She would zoom around, wagging her tail and periodically look back at Dirk, panting so hard she appeared to wave at him with her tongue. He smiled to himself as he watched her play.

Dirk always felt confident with Mollie in these fields. They were vast, covering two football pitches, and they were quite open, so he could easily spot when another dog that Mollie might be more interested in came along. It was also the place where Dirk and Mollie came for their dog training classes. Dirk always found a certain sense of comfort in that familiarity.

Mollie had learned a lot since starting her training. When Dirk first brought her home, she hadn't learned any commands, not even 'sit'. Mollie – and what she represented – meant a lot to Dirk, so he took his responsibility as her owner very seriously. He wanted to give her the best chance of a good life, and, not having had a dog before, he knew training her was well outside his skill set. After some attempts at following confusing YouTube videos, which seemed to be telling him how to do the same thing in very different ways, he decided to enlist the help of a professional.

He found a local training class and attended it every Saturday morning. Teaching Mollie the basics was important, and he also thought it was a good way to socialise with other dogs, although in reality she got super-excited and sometimes struggled to remember things she was taught. So he found more success by working one-on-one with a trainer, but still went to the classes socially. Although he was generally a loner, Dirk enjoyed meeting other people who were just as crazy about their dogs as he was. There was a real sense of community that surprised him. But he got the greatest sense of satisfaction by watching Mollie learn things.

Dirk hadn't really thought about 'how' dogs learn before, just 'what' he needed to do to get Mollie to learn. But once he understood her learning process better, the 'what' started to make more sense.

How dogs learn

One of the main ways that dogs learn is through 'association'. In other words, they learn by making links between things that they experience. For instance, they associate the sight of their bowl with being fed. Indeed, it didn't take long for Mollie to start to drool expectantly at the mere sound of the dog bowl clattering around the worktop. This is an example of one of several types of conditioning that dogs use to learn, called *Pavlovian conditioning*.

Ivan Pavlov was a Russian psychologist who, in the 1890s, carried out research into the digestive glands in dogs. The details of his experiments are quite gory, and his unpalatable methods are often skimmed over when recounted. He removed parts of the dog's oesophagus so food would fall out before it hit the stomach. Tubes attached to small holes further along the digestive tract allowed him to measure the gastric juices the dog produced.

Quite by accident, he realised that the dogs had started to drool before they saw the food when they heard the footsteps of whoever was coming to feed them. Pavlov began to ring a bell right before the dogs received their food. Over time, he found they would start to salivate as soon as they heard the bell, even when there was no food. The link between the bell and salivating had become 'conditioned'. The sound of the bell (the stimulus) became 'associated' with the food (the outcome), prompting the dogs to salivate in anticipation. It is a bit like when the bell goes at the end of class, and kids get a hit of adrenaline in anticipation of break time.

Mollie's trainer showed Dirk a training technique using a *bridge command* that used Pavlovian conditioning to help teach Mollie new things. The bridge command was the word 'good', and it 'bridged' the gap between her doing something right and a treat being delivered.

The trainer taught Dirk to 'charge' the word with a positive association by saying 'good' and giving Mollie a treat immediately after. He did this repeatedly, so Mollie formed a Pavlovian association between the sound of the word 'good' and receiving a treat. Before long, 'good' represented a treat in Mollie's mind, and she knew the piece of food would soon follow.

This short cut between the word 'good' and a treat would be important in helping Mollie form a different association. This time, it would be a link between something Mollie had just done (a response), like sitting, and receiving a treat (an outcome). This kind of association is called an *instrumental association*. That's because the dog's *response* is *instrumental* to the outcome.

When the dog hears the word 'good', it thinks that the last thing it did was the reason it got the treat. I do X and, therefore, get Y. For example, I sat on command and got a treat. For this association to form, Mollie must get the outcome within a second or so of the response. So, the trainer uses 'good' to 'mark' the correct response quickly to signal that the treat is coming. The word 'good' represents the outcome of the treat, allowing the response to link to the outcome. The dog thinks, if I sit, then I'll get a snack.

In the case of learning how to sit on command, the outcome of a treat is pleasant, making Mollie more likely to repeat the response to get more treats. But instrumental associations work the other way, too. Mollie once tried to jump up onto the kitchen worktop to get to some food scraps. She couldn't quite reach it and mistakenly pawed at a pile of delicately balanced saucepans that then fell on her. The response of jumping on the counter became quickly paired with the discomfort of a heavy pan on the head, and funnily enough, Mollie didn't repeat the behaviour. A response that's paired with an unpleasant experience makes the dog less likely to repeat it. This can also be conditioned in dogs and linked with a cue: similar to 'good' meaning a reward is coming, another word could signal something bad might happen. For example, when someone shouts 'duck', you duck without asking 'why?' a second time. The first unpleasant experience was enough!

A similar technique can be used to train dogs not to repeat a problematic or dangerous behaviour. Dogs use this learning with each other all the time. Dirk was once in a pub with Mollie, who was quietly chewing on a bone. The landlord's dog trotted up and tried to take it, and Mollie responded with a firm snap. The other dog withdrew sharply, gave a slight wince, and trotted away, having learned that particular behaviour was out of order. It was Mollie's way of telling it not to do that. For us and our dogs, it can be as simple as telling it off with a firm 'no' or a pop on the lead. Any technique to correct a dog's behaviour should always be applied by someone with experience. It can be easy to misapply this, especially if the timing is out, ending up with your dog becoming confused if it doesn't understand what it's done wrong.

As humans, we have the luxury of being able to tell someone how we feel about something and why we don't want them to do it again. Dogs can't do this and rely on giving each other outcomes to stop something from being repeated. This is a key part of how dogs communicate and live in social groups. We always focus on what we need to teach our dogs to do, but it is just as important to teach your dog what *not* to do to enable it to live safely in a human world.

Dirk often wished he could speak to Mollie and wondered what she would say back. So often he found himself repeating the same thing to her in the hope she would listen. Clearly, he still had some work to do on his communication skills because Mollie hadn't changed her associations! Nevertheless, he smiled as he watched Mollie run around the field, enjoying her freedom. Every so often, she would glance back at him to check in, panting lightly with a flash of pink tongue hanging from the left-hand side of her mouth. Her typical toothy Staffordshire Bull Terrier grin made her look more like a Cheshire cat than a dog.

Mollie put her nose to the ground and started sniffing the grass, wagging her tail happily as she trotted away from Dirk. Whatever scent she followed led her to the long grass on the edge of the field. Beyond were a few trees and scrappy-looking nettles alongside an old, rusty chicken-wire fence.

Within a few seconds, Mollie was in the bushes, exploring the hedgerow jungle with her nose. Dirk remembered the last time she did that, when she came out with half a putrid rat corpse in her mouth, so he decided to call her back to limit the risk of a repeat.

'Mollie, come!' he hollered.

Immediately, he saw the shrubbery rattle . . . and out leapt Mollie.

'Good girl!' he shouted as she came bounding over, with such enthusiasm that Dirk was surprised she didn't trip on her tongue. She came directly to his feet and plonked herself in a sitting position right before him. She looked up at him expectantly, excited for her impending treat. Dirk pulled a chunk of cheese from a bag of scraps in his pocket. The cheese was her favourite. Their trainer had always encouraged Dirk to use treats that Mollie really liked when he practised recalling her, so she would associate coming back with getting something of high value. That makes it more likely she'll be enthusiastic about coming back.

Even though Dirk felt confident on the field, given it was where he and Mollie worked with their trainer, he still felt a little gush of pride whenever she listened to him so well. It was his first experience of working with a trainer. Although he was a little sceptical at first, he'd seen the investment pay off in terms of her obedience and their relationship. Once he understood how she learns, he was better able to communicate with her in a way that she understands as well.

Dirk and Mollie moved on from the field. He decided to put her back on the lead while they walked along the path by a canal. A pair of ducks and their chicks paddled along the middle of the waterway. Dirk watched as a duckling chased a small piece of soggy bread that had broken up on the water's surface. Mollie was quite happy, trotting alongside Dirk while they soaked up their surroundings and enjoyed the mild spring sunshine.

Around a mile down the canal, they approached an old, heavy, wrought-iron gate that led to a little patch of forestry. Dirk gave the gate a shove with his shoulder and led Mollie through. They hadn't been this way before, and Dirk was looking forward to exploring, Mollie even more so. An odorous bouquet hit the olfactory receptors in her nose from every angle, and she couldn't wait to get off the lead and hunt out whatever treasures this adventure might offer. She wagged her tail and pulled on the lead as Dirk paused to shut the gate before he unclipped her.

Mollie was straight off, sniffing at everything. The trees smelled great. The little weeds smelled great. The scent of stale rabbit pee smelled divine. Mollie was busily exploring with her nose when Dirk noticed another dog and its owner, walking on the lead a little way ahead, coming towards them. Always aware of other dogs and how they might react, he called Mollie back to pop her on the lead out of courtesy. Even if Mollie was friendly and just wanted to say hello, there's no way of knowing how the other dog might react. It might be fearful, anxious or even aggressive. Its owner might have been working hard on its manners, and Dirk didn't want to undo any progress through a well-intentioned but uncontrolled interaction with his dog.

'Mollie, come!' he shouted. Mollie carried on trotting around and sniffing everything in front of her snout. Dirk sighed. Maybe she didn't hear him. He tried again.

'Mollie, come! Mollie!' he shouted, a little louder this time – still nothing.

'Mollie, come! Come, Mollie! For crying out loud, Mollie . . . come!' he shouted, more animated this time and a little more nervous, but still to no avail. He continued calling, getting increasingly irked as she continued to blank him.

'Mollie! Fucking hell. Mollie! Mooooooooolllliiiieee!' he yelled. 'Oh bollocks to it, I'm coming to get you!' he exclaimed, exasperated as he marched over to get her, her tail still wagging, nose-deep in some piddle-covered bushes.

Like many of us mere mortals, Dirk found it incredibly frustrating that his dog ignored him. After all, it's not like she didn't know what 'come' meant. She had just responded to the same command in the field, not more than ten minutes earlier. It would be easy for Dirk to assume that Mollie was wilfully blanking him, being so interested in her surroundings that he became irrelevant. However, this view would overlook some crucial aspects of how dogs learn.

When a dog learns that responding to a command leads to a reward in one place, in most cases it doesn't automatically transfer that outcome to another place. If you were to teach a dog to sit in your living room, it wouldn't automatically understand how to respond to 'sit' in the garden. The contexts differ, and dogs and many other animals experience the *context shift effect*.[1] They learn how to do something in one place (or context) but then don't know how to do it in another place. It's like teaching someone to sit on a chair in one room. But imagine that person doesn't understand what a chair, or sitting, is. They've only learned 'sitting' to mean on that one object in that one room. So when you move to another room, you must re-teach them how to sit on a new chair in different surroundings. You might have to teach them to sit on several other chairs in different rooms before they fully understand how to sit on a chair – you have to *generalise* the concept.

When dogs learn to do something, they often don't have any abstract concept of what they've just learned. They simply learn what behaviour to do, what triggers that behaviour, what they get for it, and in what context the whole learning experience took place. It's like only remembering a lesson when you're back in the classroom where you were taught. And this doesn't just apply to dogs. Killer whales moved from one facility to another seem to forget tricks they've previously learned too.[2] It wasn't that they'd had a sudden bout of amnesia or were protesting their new quarters. Instead, this was the context shift effect in action.

In Mollie's case, during her training classes, she learned that returning to Dirk when he shouted 'come!' would lead to a reward. She had learned that in the context of the field. That's why it was easy for her to compute that 'come' meant she should return to Dirk on their walk in the field. But they hadn't practised anywhere else. When Dirk tried to recall Mollie in the forest, it wasn't that she was wilfully ignoring him. It was because she'd never learned that 'come' meant the same thing anywhere else. She didn't connect the dots and didn't think Dirk wanted her to do anything, so she went blissfully about her business, wondering why Dirk was getting so agitated. If she had understood what he wanted, she certainly would have responded. Of course, it could also be that she was simply more motivated by the new smells than the idea of the reward she would expect for recall, but given her lack of generalisation work, it was most likely the former explanation.

Mollie was a happy dog and keen to please Dirk. She felt unsettled when he was so cross and didn't understand why. Dogs always do best when they can predict outcomes, and she couldn't predict this because she didn't know what he expected of her. It wasn't deliberate. It was a translation error.

This alone was frustrating, but how Dirk responded here was also important. Dirk did the obvious thing when Mollie didn't react to him recalling her, which was to recall her again. And again. And again. To be fair to Dirk, this was the intuitive thing to do. The problem is that every time he called her using the command 'come', that didn't result in Mollie coming and claiming her subsequent reward, that association between 'come' and returning to Dirk weakened. In psychological terms, there was an 'extinction' of the association between 'come' and returning to get a treat.

In reality, that meant that Mollie didn't learn what Dirk expected when he shouted 'come' as well – it's a bit like telling a child to clean their room but with no consequences for not doing it. The nagging becomes white noise and the child continues to ignore it. 'Clean your room' is no longer associated with a telling off. The link between the phrase and the concept it represents becomes weakened and eventually is extinguished. In the case of a dog, it would no longer perform the behaviour expected when the command is used. Dirk would have been far better off just clipping Mollie back on the lead calmly and carrying on with his walk. He could have started practising her recall again after a few days without letting her off the lead, so she didn't have a chance to choose not to come when called and thus turn a one-off incident into a habit.

The context Mollie learned in wasn't the only way that her understanding of what Dirk expected of her became muddied. It took Dirk a while to consistently teach her to 'sit' on command. This sounds really simple, and she always obeyed when Dirk was alone with her. But Dirk found that when he tried to get her to sit in front of other people, she wouldn't always do it. Sometimes she would, perfectly, but other times she would just look up at him, with her big, brown eyes and Staffie smile, wagging her tail. It was like he was suddenly speaking a different language. He was using the same word – 'sit' – and expected the same response from her. He was puzzled by her response, or rather her lack of one.

Now we know what we know about context specificity, it would be easy to assume that it was just that. Mollie hadn't practised 'sit' in enough places to generally link the word 'sit' with the meaning of sitting. But she was even inconsistent in their living room.

Once, Dirk's brother came to visit, and Dirk wanted to show him how clever Mollie was. When Dirk looked to his brother, grinning, and told Mollie to 'sit', he was quickly embarrassed as Mollie totally blanked him and instead rubbed up against his leg, angling for scratches.

Like all animals, Mollie would notice some things more than others when she was learning something new. Mollie particularly focused on things she could see over those she could hear. This meant that she would be more likely to process those things more keenly and would link them to whatever it was she was learning. In psychology, this concept is called *overshadowing*. The presence of a more noticeable stimulus (like one Mollie can see) makes it harder to learn about the less noticeable stimulus (like one Mollie can hear).

Research has shown this is common when training a dog, where a visual cue can easily overshadow a verbal cue if both happen together, particularly if the visual cue is more prominent or consistent.[3] Selina Gibsone from the School of Psychology at the University of Southampton worked with a team of scientists from New Zealand and Australia to look at this from the perspective of training assistance dogs, where dogs might eventually need to respond to just one aspect of a trained cue if their handler's physical abilities deteriorate.

The scientists trained sixteen dogs to touch a cup on command, combining hand and voice signals. They tested the dogs on how well they learned to perform with the combined signals, as well as with voice and hand signals individually. The study found that most dogs preferred one type of signal, with 75 per cent preferring auditory and 25 per cent preferring visual. This finding shows how easily dogs can focus on part of the picture, which can overshadow the elements we think we're presenting.

When Dirk was teaching Mollie to sit, every time he said the word 'sit', he would simultaneously use his finger in one smooth downwards motion, from pointing towards the ceiling to pointing directly at her, in unison with verbalising the command. The pointing *over-shadowed* the word. Dirk thought he was teaching Mollie to respond to the word 'sit'. In contrast, Mollie responded to the movement of his finger, believing that was the signal to sit. When Dirk tried to get Mollie to sit in front of other people, he didn't use his finger. Instead, he was so focused on the command that he would overemphasise the word. Hence, Mollie thought there was nothing to respond to. The difference was so subtle Dirk didn't even realise he was doing anything differently. Again, Mollie wasn't ignoring Dirk. She hadn't learned the same part of the lesson that Dirk thought he was teaching. Simply put, don't say and do something simultaneously if you want to teach your dog something new. Say the command, lure them with your gestures and then give the reward.

Even when your dog has thoroughly learned something, other brain processes can hinder your ability to communicate with it. Dirk had noticed that if Mollie was excited or stressed, getting her to listen to a command was virtually impossible. For example, even in the field where her recall was brilliant, if she saw a squirrel, she would be so excited to chase it that he could call her over and over again, and she wouldn't respond. Not unlike the viral video of Fenton, the dog in one of London's Royal Parks, gleefully chasing a herd of deer while his increasingly desperate owner screams, 'Feeeentooooon! Jesus Christ, Jeeeesus Chriiist' at higher and higher decibels, to absolutely no avail.

Competing with stress

Excitement and stress lead to similar physiological responses in the brain and body.[4] Information absorbed through the senses gets processed in the brain. A small, almond-shaped nugget near the base of the brain called the *amygdala* is associated with emotional processing. It interprets the information, flags it as distressing and signals the *hypothalamus* to act. The hypothalamus triggers the release of adrenaline through the *pituitary gland*, which is a pea-sized structure near the bottom of the brain. Adrenaline makes the heart pump faster, so blood and oxygen get to the muscles quicker in case you need to flee or fight the impending danger.

The stress response is controlled by the *hypothalamic-pituitary-adrenal* (HPA) axis, using various hormones to trigger the release of chemicals like cortisol, which is a steroid hormone that affects the way your body and brain metabolise energy and slows functions that aren't essential during fight or flight. When an animal or even a person is experiencing a lot of arousal – whether through excitement or stress – their bodies release cortisol and adrenaline.

Studies have found that stress can lead to deactivation in parts of the brain involved in decision-making and thinking, like the prefrontal cortex.[5] In particular, a subregion called the *dorsolateral prefrontal cortex* is very sensitive to stress. This part of the brain is involved with executive functions (such as directing attention and self-control, planning what to do, working memory, etc). It has receptors that stress hormones can bind to. This alters how the brain cells fire, meaning the brain has fewer resources available to process information.

When new information presents itself in this environment, it is harder for the brain to register something it should give attention to as information competes for restricted processing resources. Some sources of information don't even register. So when Mollie was blissfully chasing a squirrel, she may have been unaware that Dirk was calling her. She could have been experiencing 'auditory exclusion'. It's akin to temporary hearing loss because Mollie can't process what, in this case, is important auditory information – Dirk's calls. Dirk hadn't realised when he arrived at the forest that Mollie's behaviour, pulling on the lead and excitedly trying to sniff everything, indicated she was too aroused by the new environment to pay attention to him. He should not have let her off the lead.

It's not only dogs that can experience this. People do, too. One study explored the impact of stress on police officers in Belgium and found similar results, noting the physical reactions they might experience under stress.[6] They included auditory exclusion, visual problems and memory loss, all linked to increased cortisol levels and an increased heartbeat. The parallels with Mollie are clear: stress increases cortisol, which shuts down parts of the brain that are important for directing attention, leading to reduced capacity to process things you see and hear, which you can't then remember.

There are ways that dogs can be trained to work in arousing or stressful environments without succumbing to their physiological responses, just like elite athletes have to learn to perform under pressure. Police and military dogs are great examples. Their handlers expose them to stressors, like loud noises or aggressive people, in a controlled way to 'habituate' them. This repeated controlled exposure results in the dogs having a significantly reduced response. It's a bit like hearing a loud noise repeatedly, but realising it doesn't have a dire consequence, leading to you no longer being afraid of it.

---

*Try this: Teach your dog a rock-solid recall**
When you call your dog back, you will compete for its attention against all kinds of things it finds more appealing. There will be exciting things it can see and smell, things it might want to chase. Your dog will find some of these activities innately rewarding at a biological level. It's like being a kid, and your

---

* Before teaching recall, it's a good idea to make sure your dog can walk to heel on the lead well. If they have a tendency to pull on the lead, work on walking to heel first. If things aren't right when they're at your feet, things won't be right when they're at a distance. Have a look at Chapter 6 for exercises to help. Similarly, if your dog is reactive or aggressive, those issues must be tackled first to keep your dog and others safe in case they respond dangerously to a trigger. See Chapter 3 for advice on this.

mum's calling you to leave the arcade when you're engrossed in a game. Playing the game is significantly more rewarding than going home with your mum. You're fighting against those instincts with your dog when you're out, and trying to get the dog to come back to you when the bushes just smell *so* good.

Before teaching your dog how to recall, figure out what motivates it. What gets it excited? Is it food or a toy? Does your dog prize interaction with you above all else? Could it be a game of tug of war? If it's food, what kind of food? Is it a bit of meat, like cooked chicken? Or cheese? Maybe a chunk of steak? Play around with different rewards and get a sense of what your dog prefers. This will be the high-value reward you use to teach it to recall. Suppose your dog isn't motivated by anything, not even tasty treats. In that case, you can experiment with using its main meals in your training sessions, instead of additional snacks that it may not have room for.

The basic premise of teaching recall is that every time you call, something good happens for your dog. We use the reward as both a 'positive reinforcer' – to reward the behaviour we want – and a 'positive interrupter' because it interrupts whatever your dog is engaged with, with something even better. But of course, the 'interruption' only happens when the distractions you're competing against hold less value than the reward you're using.

So, start in a familiar environment, like at home or in your garden, where there are less likely to be lots of new smells and distractions. Have your high-value reward ready and put your dog on a lead so you can eradicate the chance of it failing the exercise by choosing not to come to you when you call it.

Use your recall word – in this case, we'll use 'come' – and, only if you need to, pull gently on the lead while you step backwards to encourage your dog to come to you. When it does, be really happy and excited. Praise your dog wildly as if it's just rescued a litter of kittens from a frozen river. Be their biggest cheerleader.

Keep practising this until your dog comes reliably and instantly without putting pressure on the lead. The stronger the association between 'come' and returning to you for fun, the more reliable its recall will be.

Not all dogs will get this right away. If your dog ignores you, try increasing the fun. If you're using a ball, bounce it. If it's a toy, shake it or make it squeak. Be louder, happier, even more excited and animated. Move like nobody's watching! If your dog is still ignoring you, use a gentle vibration pressure on the lead – use quick, gentle pulses to get its attention. Don't pull the dog towards you. As soon as your dog looks at you, stop pulsing the lead and run backwards to encourage it to come to you. Reward it as soon as it gets to you. If you're using a bridge command like we discussed in Chapter 1, mark with a 'yes' as soon as your dog makes eye contact with you.

Keep doing this and, gradually, hold off the mark until your dog approaches you, as it gets more skilled in the exercise. In the first stage, you're rewarding your dog for breaking its attention with the environment, and working towards rewarding it when it gets to you. The attention part of the exercise becomes part of the conditioned response, and the reward is payment for moving from wherever it is to wherever you are.

Once your dog understands this in a distraction-free environment on a short lead, progress to letting it engage with its surroundings a bit more before you recall it. For example, let it sniff around in the bushes and then call it back so that it's breaking its attention to return. Don't overdo this, though, or your dog might not want to leave your side because it knows you're a walking treat dispenser! Keep it fresh and vary the rhythm so your dog doesn't start to predict what's coming. Otherwise you'll get a false positive – you'll think your dog is responding to the recall but really it's become conditioned to you and that environment.

That brings us on to our next step. Repeat this in a range of environments so your dog starts to 'generalise' the concept. This avoids the context shift effect. Try recalling it when you're out and about for a walk, practise it in the park, and do it in dog-friendly cafés and car parks. When you're generalising, it's essential to think about those contexts. Think about the ground – different floors will feel different to your dog. Practise it on pavements, wood chips, grass, tiles, wooden floors, long grass and mud. Everything you can think of.

Once your dog can respond consistently on a short lead in various environments, you are ready to increase the distance. We take a few steps back whenever we progress to something new, simplifying the environment to set our dogs up to succeed.

Go back to a relatively distraction-free environment and put your dog on a long line. This is a long lead – it can be about 20 metres – and it means that your dog can move further away from you while you still have control of it. You can use lead pressure to direct it towards you if it fails to respond to your recall word.

Start to practise recalling your dog when connected to the long line, gradually increasing the distance you call it from. Do this in precisely the same way that you did on the short lead. Now that your dog is coming from further away, it's time to ramp up the excitability factor. Your enthusiasm here is critical. The more effort you put in, the stronger your recall will be. If you make it fun and exciting to come back to you, your dog will run back quickly, ignoring distractions. You might even trigger your dog's prey drive if it thinks it's coming to play with a toy, which is a powerful instinct to employ in your favour.

If you're not so excited, your dog might mosey back but will be more susceptible to distractions on the way. Only reward your dog when it gets to you. And again, repeat this across various environments so your dog generalises the recall.

The next stage is tricky and can easily go wrong. You are going to start to practise recalling in the face of distractions. By now, you will have worked out what makes your dog tick. If it's a big foodie, and you want to use food as a distraction, you might begin with a little pile of plain food like dry kibble dropped on the floor. If it loves toys, you might try putting a ball on the ground nearby. Just ensure that *your* reward is of higher value – the concept is that you and whatever you have hold more value than the distraction. And also make sure that your lead isn't so long that it can reach it and fail the game. Allow your dog to move towards the distraction and recall it before it gets so close to it that it ignores you. This will help you establish your dog's 'threshold', i.e. how close it can get before it ignores your recall and goes for the distraction.

Gradually allow it to move closer to the distraction before you recall it, until you are confident that it will come back to you. Then repeat this in numerous environments. Look for different distractions that you can practise recalling your dog from. Every time you do this, you will reinforce that returning to you is much more enjoyable than anything else that might catch its attention.

Once you're satisfied that your dog understands the concept of coming back, it must learn that coming back isn't a choice.

It's a must. Recall is vital for your dog's safety. It can prevent it from running into roads, chasing livestock or getting too close to another dog, which could result in a dog fight.

When your dog goes past its threshold and ignores its recall word, you need to help it learn it is better not to. Give a short, sharp pop on the lead to disrupt it. As soon as it looks at you, use your verbal mark – draw it in by your excitability. Don't repeat your recall word to keep the command clear. The pop should not be continuous pressure on the lead, which can trigger a dog's 'opposition reflex' (where it automatically pulls in the opposite direction). It's simply a quick pop to get its attention and bring in the fun.

The dog associates coming back with all manner of fun, and ignoring the command with an unpleasant (but not painful) sensation. Only do this once the dog understands what it *should* do, never when the dog hasn't learned the concept, as it will not understand what behaviour it *should not* have done.

Continue practising this in many different environments against many other distractions. Keep practising until your dog returns consistently, getting closer and closer to distracting things. If you find you are continuingly popping the lead, you might consider working with a trainer. Popping the lead should reduce the likelihood of a behaviour recurring. If this isn't occurring, a professional can help you to understand what might be happening. Timing and technique are really important here, and they can guide you through this if you need a little more help.

If you wish, you can proof-test this exercise with a 50-metre line until your dog's recall is solid. However, you might have noticed that your dog is sensitive to when it is attached to the long line and when it is unclipped. Some dogs will be very wise to this: when they hear the lead being unclipped, they shoot off and start to ignore your calls, knowing that you're not able to grab a lead and stop them from running away. If your dog falls into this camp, clip on a second light lead, and continue practising with both leads attached. After a while, try unclipping one lead and continuing your practice. Your dog will quickly learn that, despite hearing the clip, it cannot ignore the recall.

When your dog is ready to progress to being recalled with no lead, return to a controlled environment with no distractions and start to practise. Gradually build up to longer distances, then different environments and distractions. If you see your dog hesitate in recalling at any point, put it back on a long line and continue practising for a week or two. Your dog must not experience success in ignoring your recall.

A final point, but perhaps the most important one. Never scold or punish your dog for not recalling or coming back too slowly. It will quickly learn that coming back to you is unpleasant and will form a negative association between the recall word and returning to you. That will undo all the good work you've put in so far. Limit yourself to a pop on the lead to interrupt your dog so it understands the ignoring is undesirable, and get it to return with excitement.

Some dogs are excessively driven by an instinct to chase – their 'prey drive'. This can differ between dogs that are bred for different purposes. For example, Border Collies are bred to herd sheep, so they have a strong innate desire to chase things. A terrier, bred to chase and hunt small mammals, will find it harder to ignore a squirrel when you call it back. Every dog has a certain level of chase instinct, which will differ on an individual basis. Even a dog that hasn't been bred for a strong prey drive can, by chance, have an incredibly powerful chase instinct. If this is the case with your dog and you're finding them too difficult to teach recall, enlist the help of a trainer with proven results with the type and temperament of dog you have.

Finally, teaching recall can be really frustrating. You're human. Don't train through this frustration because it will interfere with the way you're interacting with your dog. Simply take your dog home and try again fresh another day. Also don't be afraid to go back a few steps in your training, especially if you had a bad experience, so you can solidify your dog's understanding. At times in Danny's career he's had to take a dog right back to 'week one, day one' in order to make sure it learns something properly. That's dog training. Focusing only on the destination makes you miss out on the journey. Enjoy the journey, and the destination will come.

Summary
- Dogs learn by association. They link either a stimulus with an outcome (Pavlovian conditioning) or a response they make with an outcome (instrumental conditioning).
- Dogs learn a positive association between something and a positive experience, making them more likely to repeat a behaviour. Dogs also learn a negative association between something and a negative experience which makes them less likely to repeat a behaviour.
- Dogs can experience the context shift effect where they learn something in one location, but it does not automatically generalise to other places.
- If you continue to use a command you have taught your dog after it has ignored you, it is possible to weaken the association between that command and the behaviour you expect from your dog. It becomes 'devalued'.
- Dogs can experience 'overshadowing' where one stimulus makes it harder to learn about a less noticeable stimulus.
- Dogs can experience 'auditory exclusion' when they are

particularly aroused or stressed, which is where their brains do not process sounds.

- Teach your dog to recall by using a high-value reward and enthusiastically calling it back to you.
- Practise initially in a distraction-free environment and build up to various other environments and distractions to enable your dog to 'generalise' the command.
- Once your dog can do this on a short lead, practise on a long lead and gradually increase the distance you recall from. Repeat the process with various distractions.
- Every time you build up to more challenging variations of the exercise, return to a distraction-free environment and build up gradually.
- Once your dog is consistently returning on a long line, practise with no lead.
- If your dog shows any hesitation, put it back on a long line and practise more.
- Never, ever scold your dog for not returning or returning too slowly.

Chapter 3

What your dog is thinking when it's watching you

Sadie heard an almighty crash coming from the living room, and the dogs barking furiously. She steadied herself against the kitchen counter and took a deep breath to prepare herself for the inevitable chaos she knew she was about to witness. Sadie turned around and reached for the door handle, wincing. She was not looking forward to what she would find on the other side.

As she opened the door, Sadie was hit by a wall of sound. Her two dogs, Milo and Hench, were barking loudly and excitedly; long, deep, continuous barks which ricocheted around the room. Neither dog came up for breath. Both were bounding up at the window, jumping back and forth in frustration, bouncing off each other as they did so. Their claws tapped at the window panes as they pawed at the glass, hoping to somehow get through this annoying invisible barrier. Then, they could protect the household from that Amazon delivery driver . . . just as they'd attempted to do with the paper boy, the postie and two Jehovah's Witnesses earlier that day.

In the chaos, the dogs had knocked over the side table. On the floor lay the remnants of a smashed plant pot, the dirt trampled into the carpet, aided by half a cup of lukewarm tea that Sadie had intended to come back and finish. Green, stringy leaves of a now tangled snake plant were strewn across the floor, the once pretty pot plant in myriad pieces under the windowsill. Snotty nose marks streaked the glass where the dogs had dragged their faces across the window. The house phone that usually sat on the table was nowhere to be seen (the dogs had probably knocked it underneath the sofa in the mêlée). Hench momentarily turned to look at Sadie with an expression that clearly said, 'You'll never believe that the plant tried to attack me, but luckily I defeated it, and I'm still alive.'

Sadie could feel the pressure building inside her as she took in the devastation, a potent combination of anger, frustration and dismay. Then she blew.

'QUIIIIIIEEET!' she screamed at the top of her lungs – but the dogs didn't even acknowledge her interruption.

'DOOOOOGS! SHUT UP, SHUT UP, SHUT UUUUUP!' she shouted desperately. She was so loud she wondered how many doors up the street would have been able to hear her – still, no response from the dogs. If anything, Milo, in particular, just seemed to bark even more. It was like a game, and he had one more player on his team.

Exasperated, Sadie grabbed Milo and Hench by their collars and dragged them away, still barking and wriggling to get free. Milo spun around and twisted his collar around her thumb, and she yelped in pain and let go. Milo ran back up to the window, barking, and Hench joined in the chorus with renewed vigour. Sadie chased after him and grabbed him again, muttering under her breath as she did so. She tripped over them constantly as she wrangled them into the kitchen, away from the window of doom, and into their individual crates for some quiet time.

Sadie sighed as she shut the crate doors. She turned around and slid down to the floor, cradling her head in her hands. She felt her eyes start to burn as she welled up and sobbed quietly into her sleeve. It wasn't supposed to be this hard. She loved her dogs, but at that moment, she also hated them. She felt conflicted and guilty because she believed you were only supposed to feel good about your dogs. And in that moment, she felt anything but good. And she had no idea what she could do to change things.

Milo and Hench weren't your typical pair. In fact, they couldn't be more different in a hundred ways. Hench was an Italian Greyhound – a very slender, thin-boned version of a Whippet. He was, in fact, anything but 'hench' (slang for muscular). When he was just a puppy, Sadie's teenage son, Ben, thought it ironic to call him Hench, given how skinny he was. Now, Ben is no longer a teenager but a thirty-one-year-old man with a job and a mortgage, and the dog's name feels a little bit silly.

Nevertheless, the name stuck around, as did Hench, now the grand old age of fourteen. His muzzle and eyebrows were white, but that somehow blended well with his dove-grey fur. His eyes were big and round, making him look like an eternal puppy. His exceptionally short coat meant he was easily cold, so he was often seen sporting a blue knitted jumper, the same shade as Paddington Bear's coat. It made him look a little bit like a teddy.

Milo, on the other hand, was a menace. He was an Australian Cattle Dog crossed with a Border Collie. He looked adorable, with a beautiful coat of grey, black and red-flex patches across his back like a saddle on an otherwise pure white body. He had gorgeous red patches over his eyes that stretched down his face. His little, wispy ears flopped to the side of his head, unless he was excited when they stood up on end.

He was a beautiful dog, but he was permanently wired. It was like he nibbled coffee beans from the moment he woke up to the moment he went to sleep. He was overly alert and would leap up at even the slightest sound. He would bark, growl and snap. Every time the doorbell rang, there was chaos. When the phone rang, he would knock it onto the floor. He had so much energy that he would even try to herd the iron, jumping back and forth every time Sadie swept it across the linen, running around the ironing board and nearly knocking her off her feet.

Sadie had thought it might be nice for Hench to have some company in his old age, so she adopted Milo from the local shelter. She didn't know much about Milo's background, but Sadie suspected that his behaviour and insatiable energy contributed to him ending up there. Determined not to give up on him, Sadie persevered . . . much to the detriment of her quality of life. And Hench's.

Being quite a sedentary soul, Hench hadn't previously shown any interest in reacting to people outside the window. Hench used to perch quietly on the chair by the window for hours, just watching the world go by without so much as a peep. It was only when Milo joined the pack and started barking at anything that passed that Hench decided to join in. Milo had shown him a new game that blew his mind, and now he can't stop playing it. (Something similar happens with teenagers and online games, apparently.)

Dogs are adept at learning from each other and show *allelomimetic behaviour*, where they copy the behaviour of others. An example would be one wolf howling and the rest of the pack joining in. Puppies as young as six weeks old have shown allelomimetic behaviour. It's a bit like contagious practical behaviour. Researchers from the Mammal Research Institute at the University of Pretoria in South Africa, and the Ethology, Zoological Institute at the University of Bonn in Germany, studied this in working dogs. They took German Shepherd pups from mothers who were trained narcotic detection dogs, and also from dogs that had never had scent detection training.[1] The pups from the detection dogs were allowed to watch their mothers at work, sniffing out narcotics packages and getting rewarded when they found them. Without any other training or reinforcement, at six months old, the pups were all tested on their ability to find hidden packages of drugs.

This test was challenging for the pups, given they hadn't been taught what to do. It would be perfectly understandable if they mooched around the place, sniffing and chewing on things while looking adorable. Surprisingly, those pups that had watched their mothers doing scent detection work when they were six to twelve weeks old were much more able to sniff out a packet of drugs than pups that hadn't observed their mothers doing the same task. They were copying their mothers.

A similar practice takes place when puppies are trained for bite sports. A puppy will be tethered and allowed to watch the older dogs as they run and attack someone on command. This serves two purposes. Firstly, it capitalises on the opportunity for the young dogs to exhibit allelomimetic behaviour and copy what they see. It also makes the youngsters excited and a little frustrated because they, too, want to join in. This increases their 'drive', or their motivation, to take part in the game.

In many ways, this is a highly adaptive quality and would have been helpful for packs of wild dogs learning to hunt. However, in Hench's case, copying Milo's chaotic behaviours was slightly more maladaptive. It created bedlam in the house. And, of course, when Sadie came into the room and started shouting at the dogs, she was quite understandably trying to get their attention and call them to stop. But from Milo and Hench's perspectives, Sadie was alerted by their calls and came and joined in. Her alarmed shouts are equivalent to their warning barks. No wonder they barked even more. They had persuaded Sadie – their very own Sadie, the controller of everything, the boss, the leader, the super sapien – to join them in their barking game. What a win! To them, Sadie was engaging in allelomimetic behaviour, taking her lead from them. They had no sense that she was asking them to stop. She was, instead, pouring fuel onto an already burning 'arousal' fire.

Milo's problem behaviour wasn't limited to the house. He was highly strung and incredibly wary of new situations. He habitually barked at buses and lorries and tried to snap at their wheels. He once pulled the lead straight out of Sadie's hand and caught the wheel of a slow-moving lorry with his jaws. The wheel spun him around and faceplanted him into the curb. He was fortunate not to have been dragged under the truck, escaping with minor cuts and bruises and a snapped canine tooth.

Sadie remembered the first time she was walking with Milo, and he saw a bus. He had stopped to sniff some graffiti pee left by another dog on the corner of the bus shelter. The bus came along the road, slowly grinding to a halt.

Sadie, wary of Milo's tendency to respond to new things by barking, was slightly anxious about the people getting off. She didn't want to be embarrassed or need to start apologising to old ladies for Milo taking a nip at their trolley bags. In a slightly high-pitched and urgent voice, she said, 'Milo, time to go. Milo! Milo!' He glanced back at her, and with that, the bus came to a halt. The air brakes let off an excruciatingly loud hiss. The tyres gave off that distinctive smell of hot tacky rubber and tarmac. Dogs have incredibly sensitive hearing (they can hear about four times better than people), and Milo had never encountered a bus next to him before.

Milo spun around and jumped, somewhat spooked by the noise and the smell. He looked back at Sadie, not quite knowing what to do. Her eyes were wide, and she looked nervous about the impending encounter. That made him more anxious – in his mind, if Sadie was afraid, he should be afraid.

Sadie pulled Milo away. As the pressure on the lead tightened, he pulled against it, turned around, and started barking at the scary-looking bus. To Milo, it was all on him now. He was the defender of both of them. He stood boldly, making himself look as big as possible, and snarled with eyes wide and ears back. He snapped and jumped back. Then he lunged forward, snapping at the tyres, then jumped back again. Just as Sadie reached out to try to soothe him, he turned around and nipped her on the arm. So she pulled him away, shouting at him instead.

Milo displayed redirected aggression. The key word here is 'redirected'. Milo didn't choose to bite Sadie; he was so hyped up that it was more like a reflex. It's a bit like if you were exploring a dark, aban-doned building with a friend and you were a little freaked out and on edge. But your friend thought hiding and jumping out at you would be funny. But you're startled, and react by shoving them away. You're not being aggressive: you're nervous, and you react without thinking. When dogs display *redirected aggression*, there is no clarity of thought. They're aroused and just respond in the same way. Although even unintentional bites can be severe.

The truth is, it wasn't just the unusual sight of the bus that triggered Milo's reaction. Like all dogs, he was highly attuned to his owner's response. In addition to allelomimetic behaviour, where dogs copy or mimic, they are capable of *social referencing*. This refers to the process where the dog would look to others to obtain information that clarifies a situation. People do this, too, especially in an ambiguous situation where you're unsure how to respond. Take, for example, going to dinner in a very posh restaurant with more knives and forks around your placemat than you think it's possible to eat with in one sitting. You may have absolutely no clue where to start, so you look around at others, hoping someone else's choices might give you a clue.

Fear spreads

Research has shown that dogs look to us to gauge what to do in a new situation, especially when they encounter something they're not sure about, just as Milo looked to Sadie for direction when he was unsure what to make of the bus. A study from researchers in Milan involving ninety dogs and their owners explored how dogs could read a human's positive or negative emotional response to a potentially scary object.[2] In this case, it was a loud fan with brightly coloured streamers attached. Each dog was brought into the room with the frightening fan. When the dog looked at the person accompanying them (either their owner or a stranger), that person responded with either a happy expression and voice or a fearful one.

The vast majority of dogs looked towards the humans when faced with an object they were unsure of. Three-quarters of dogs looked to their owners, and only slightly fewer, 60 per cent, looked towards a stranger in the room to take a cue in an uncertain situation. When owners, in particular, were optimistic about the situation, dogs were more attentive. They approached the object more readily than those whose owners were more negative about it. There were fewer behavioural differences when the stranger gave the cues, despite the dogs still referring to them. So, the closer the relationship, the more trusting dogs are of social cues. Either way, they are susceptible to our actions when deciding whether something is a threat.

In the scenario with the bus, Milo looked to Sadie for a clue because he was unsure about the situation. When Sadie looked anxious – albeit due to her anticipation of his reaction – he read that as a cue that the problem was potentially dangerous. That, coupled with her response being to flee by pulling him away, signalled to him that he should be wary of the imminent danger. That's why he started to lunge and snap at the bus; he couldn't relate to it, so he attempted to scare it away and create space.* And when he felt the collar pull in one direction, his innate response was to push against it (opposition reflex), contributing to his reaction. When the bus pulled away, Milo perceived this as a victory, so he thought the behaviour was a good strategy, and it stuck.

Since that encounter, Milo sees buses – and lorries, as they look similar – as deadly road wagons that must be frightened off by any means necessary. Which, to him, means snapping with his three-and-a-half canines. His perspective was triggered and reinforced by his take on Sadie's nervous response to the scary thing.

* In this case, Milo was reacting out of fear. Many Collies may do something similar because they have a strong genetic tendency to herd things.

The thing is, whenever Milo does try to scare off the dangerous objects, they disappear a few short seconds later. So, as far as he's concerned, his snapping and barking works. He then experiences a sense of success and relief, which releases brain chemicals like dopamine and triggers activity in his caudate nucleus – his brain's reward centre – and he feels pretty good. It's a bit like when someone starts harassing you in the street, and you tell them to go away, then – somewhat miraculously – they do. You feel good, not least because your response is validated by a successful outcome.

Dogs experience the same when they attempt to create space by snapping and barking, even when out of fear, and then the frightening person or thing does indeed leave. Milo and Hench experience something similar when they bark at people passing the window. They bark because they see a threat; the threat (who is just minding their own business and passing by) disappears, and in this case, the dogs see that outcome as a result of their actions. They see it as a successful strategy and are more likely to continue performing that same behaviour every time they see someone walk past their window. Eventually, this kind of behaviour can become *self-reinforcing*. In other words, the act itself feels so good that it becomes the reward.

Sadie began to dread taking Milo on walks and certainly couldn't handle the stress of taking him and Hench out together. Whenever she spotted oncoming traffic, she would tense up and take a sharp breath. Sadie became anxious, knowing it was going to be embarrassing. She dreaded people's judgemental looks, glaring at her because she couldn't handle her dog. She even wondered why she had Milo and felt ashamed that she couldn't control him better.

The truth is, Sadie was being unfairly hard on herself. It's common for dogs to react to their environment, and Milo was particularly reactive. His mix of Border Collie and Australian Cattle Dog meant that he was genetically predisposed to having lots of energy and being very alert. It was little wonder that he was easily spooked; he was wired to be particularly attuned to the environment. Because he was anxious, he would look to her to show him it was OK. But when she looked nervous, too, he would respond by barking to create space and get the threat to go away. And when he did kick off, Sadie would move him in another direction. The threat was no longer there, and he figured all he had to do to get back to feeling safe was to bark and react. It became a strategy that worked.

Dogs feel it before they see it

A dog's emotional response to something can start much earlier than we begin to notice. One fMRI study looked at the activity in the brains of thirteen dogs in a situation designed to make them cross, by seeing their owner interacting with another dog.[3]

Peter Cook, Ashley Prichard, Mark Spivak and Gregory Berns ran the study with dogs in the USA. Each dog was trained to sit perfectly still in the brain scanner while their human put on a well-choreographed show directly in their eyeline. A life-sized and realistic stuffed dog sat in front of them, looking up at their human, who was either popping tasty treats in their mouth or dropping treats in a bucket. The idea is that seeing another dog being fed by *their* human would make them angry because they want to guard access to their owner, whom they see as their social resource. The bucket was there as a control. If the dog was bothered by the food going in the bucket as well as being 'fed' to the stuffed dog, it would be because they wanted the food. If they were only bothered about it going to the other dog, it would suggest they didn't want to share their owner.

The study found that dogs prone to responding aggressively had more activation in the amygdala – a part of the brain that has a role in signalling fear – when their owners were feeding another dog in front of them. But crucially, they saw activation in this area even without any aggressive behaviours from the dog. This suggests that dogs might feel like reacting well before we see any sign of it that we might then respond to. Our dogs are always watching us, and they certainly start to feel triggered before we notice any sign that things are about to go downhill very quickly. Coupled with their sensitivity to our reaction, it's entirely plausible that our dogs might feel anxious and take a cue about the situation from our behaviour well before we notice any change in them.

Sadie had often thought that Milo was quite an aggressive dog. He would only have to see a bus out of the corner of his eye for him to tense up. He would stare in the direction of the bus and his ears would stand up on end, the pointy tips making them look like antennae. Then his body would stiffen up, and he would lean into the lead. And before she knew it, he was at the end of the lead, dragging her towards the vehicle as if he was a boxer losing it with their opponent at a particularly sparky weigh-in.

In truth, Sadie's perspective seems perfectly intuitive. Her dog is trying to attack the bus by barking and snapping. Of course he looks aggressive. But the reality is slightly more nuanced.

Milo was highly attuned to the environment and wasn't very confident. He was nervous. Everything felt like it could be a threat. The buses and lorries were scary, that's why he chased them. The sound of the wind through the trees was alarming – he didn't know whether it signalled something might attack them, and it put him on high alert. That crisp packet blowing across their path was frightening. I mean, who's to say it wasn't sheltering some poltergeist that would scrunch up him and Sadie and put them into the packet? Bikes were scary too – what if they sting if they touch you?

Milo was scared, so although he looked aggressive, his reaction was defensive. He wanted to make the scary thing disappear, so he would bark at it to frighten it off. If he looked like he would attack it, perhaps it would leave them alone. And whenever Milo did, and the bus disappeared down the road, or the potential intruder went past the window and didn't stop, it felt like a win. The aggressive behaviour – that stemmed from fear – created space and got rid of the scary thing, and Milo instantly felt better. He realised this was a good strategy – for him, at least. Poor Sadie would disagree, though. She was nearing her wits' end. She found it hugely embarrassing and hated the judgemental looks she got from other people when Milo bounced around like a killer Tigger at the end of the lead.

Reading cues gives clues

To be fair to Sadie, she was by no means alone in her misperception of Milo's behaviour. Research from Columbia University in New York City has found that it's not uncommon for people to misinterpret fearful behaviours.[4] More than two thousand people with varying experiences with dogs participated in the study. This ranged from people with zero experience with dogs (otherwise known as 'cat people') to dog owners and professionals who worked with dogs daily.

Each person watched videos of dogs displaying happy or fearful behaviour, with no other context given. Based solely on the dogs' behaviour, people could not consistently identify whether the dogs were fearful. The likelihood of getting this right increased dramatically with experience, which might not be surprising. However, it was shocking how difficult it was for the layperson to spot correctly when a dog was afraid.

Another study that scanned people's brains when they were looking at dogs interacting found differences in brain activity between dog experts and other people.[5] They were interested in activity in the *posterior superior temporal sulcus* (pSTS), which has a role in processing and reasoning in relation to social interactions and intentions that trigger them.

When looking at two dogs interacting, dog experts had similar brain patterns in the pSTS as when two humans interacted. Non-experts only had this activity when looking at humans. This suggested that dog experts interpreted how dogs' bodies were positioned as non-verbal cues to give social information in the same way as they would with people. Laypeople didn't have this ability, so it shows that understanding how dogs behave can take a lot of experience.

Looking at the position of a single body part isn't enough; instead, the combination of how the body is held and the way a dog moves is key in determining the reason for the response. Sadie was being unfairly hard on herself. Most people with a pet dog won't have the expert experience to understand the intricacies of a dog's interactions, how they respond to a situation, or, in Milo's case, the subtle differences between aggression and fear.

Since Sadie couldn't read Milo's nuanced cues to understand that he was afraid, she didn't respond as she might if she had understood the reasons for his behaviour. And remember, dogs are always reading us. Whenever Sadie saw a bus or lorry in the distance, she would tense up and tighten her grip on the lead in anticipation of Milo blowing up. Milo would constantly read Sadie and always notice her tensing up, which was his cue that danger was imminent.

Dogs can also use their sense of smell to tell our mood and respond to it accordingly.[6] When people sweat, they give off *chemosignals* (chemical messengers) that smell different, depending on their feelings. When one human smells another human's chemosignals, it triggers a *simulacrum* or a mental representation of whatever emotion the sweater felt when sweating. It's a way of subconsciously transmitting how we feel to others. And it's relevant for the dogs around us too.

The dog experts running this particular study wanted to see if dogs were sensitive to human chemosignals. The researchers harvested sweat from people wearing absorbent pads under their armpits while they watched a video that made them happy, or a film they found terrifying. These pads then went off to the lab, to be combined into super-sweat samples provided by several people.

Scientists presented the sweat pads to dogs in a room, and incredibly, they affected how the dogs behaved. When they could smell 'fear' sweat, dogs showed signs of stress and returned to their owner for comfort. Female dogs were particularly sensitive and were also more likely to try and interact with a stranger over their owner when they could smell happy sweat. The chemosignals were driving a type of synchrony between the brains of dogs and humans.

Not only are dogs capable of the same mental representations of mood driven by the smell of chemosignals, but they are also capable of doing it across species – with humans. Your mood can very clearly affect the way your dog is behaving.

In Sadie's case, her fear of how Milo would respond was likely impacting her chemosignals, which would, in turn, make Milo more anxious. He would start to gear himself up for the impending interaction. He would be more alert, look around for the trigger, and then stiffen up and lock on to his target. Then he would fixate, lick his lips a little, and whine. Then, as sure as eggs are eggs, he would lunge aggressively and bark loudly to scare away the threat. Sadie would shout at him (i.e. she would join in, in his eyes) until she managed to tug him away, and the trigger disappeared. Thus, Milo successfully distanced them from the killer threat – usually a bus – keeping him and his human safe from danger. Mission accomplished.

Milo tended to respond with problematic behaviours, but, like all dogs, he took his cue from those around him. He was mistaking Sadie's anxiety about his reaction for anxiety about the situation. And that, to him, was enough to warrant his overblown response. As social animals, our dogs are always watching us. We are a key reference point for their social behaviours, and our responses to them are much more powerful than we might think.

Try this: Prevent your dog from copying bad habits
Now that we know that our dogs' behaviours are heavily
influenced by what other people and dogs do in their presence,
we can start to think about how we can control the
environment to prevent them from picking up bad habits
through allelomimetic behaviour.

Dogs can learn behaviours from other dogs. This is
especially important to bear in mind if you already have a
dog and plan to bring another into your household. This is
equally relevant if you decide to dog-sit someone else's dog,
or even regularly walk your dog with another person and
their dog. The basic premise is to control the environment,
so your dog isn't exposed to behaviours you don't want it to
pick up.

To make this easier, you can do some pre-planning. If you
are bringing a new dog into the home, keep the dogs separate
at first so you can observe the new dog for a while and list
any behaviours that you don't want your other dog to pick
up. You can also use that list to devise a training programme
to work through those issues later. For now, we'll focus on
how to prevent those habits from spreading to your other
dog.

Hench started copying Milo's bad behaviours when they
were left alone, freely roaming the house. A simple way to
prevent this is to ensure both dogs are crate trained (see
Chapter 2) and to leave them in separate crates whenever you
leave the house. If the problem behaviours include barking,
locate the crates in different parts of the house where they're
out of earshot if possible.

Ideally, bring one dog out at a time for one-on-one
interaction with you until you've dealt with the problem
behaviours on your list. This has the additional benefit of

extra-focused bonding time with your new dog, and reinforcing that bond with your existing dog.

Remember, the more behaviours are practised, the more likely they will stick. Keep a house lead on your new dog, so if you spot it doing something you don't want to become a habit, you can use the lead to guide it away from mischief.

Given how easily Hench picked up Milo's bad habits in the house, Sadie was right not to walk them together. She might have found Hench starting to react to things in the same way as Milo. If you decide to walk your dog with another dog, be mindful of their habits. If you have a particularly reactive dog, deal with those behaviours before you start going on a pack walk together.

Remember that with any new addition, the dog must develop a bond with you first and foremost. Your objective is for it to look to you for guidance and instruction. This will be inhibited if you walk with other dogs first. Spend one-on-one time with your new dog to establish that relationship, ensuring it looks to you – not another dog – for direction.

No matter how well trained another dog may be, its instinct will always be to behave like a dog. You may not always be able to guarantee they'll respond to each other in a way that is in line with your expectations. So build that bond first, ensure your new dog is trained in line with your training objectives, and then enjoy spending time with both your dogs.

Try this: Teach your dog – and yourself – to respond differently
When we try to deal with fear-based behaviours like Milo's, we also need to think about how the behaviours of the person at the other end of the lead might contribute to the problem. This exercise will help you work through teaching your dog to respond differently to something it finds triggering, while also

training yourself to be mindful of how you respond. It is based on the behaviour modification technique of *counter-conditioning*, which means replacing an unwanted behaviour triggered by a stimulus with a new response. This kind of counter-conditioning is most effective when dealing with fear-based behaviours.

To do this, we will be talking about *threshold*. Your dog's threshold is like an emotional breaking point. It's the limit it can reach before it reacts to something. Take Milo, for example. His threshold is dictated by how far away the bus (or stimulus) is, and how long he is exposed to it – he might tolerate a second or two, but any longer can result in a reaction. It can also be affected by the strength of the stimulus – for instance, a stationary bus might be more tolerable than a moving one, or vice versa.

The first step is to establish your dog's threshold for the trigger. Set up a scenario where the trigger is present, and you can control the distance between your dog and the trigger. If it's a bus, find a parked bus in a depot at a quiet time of day. If it is another dog, ask a friend to help you by bringing their dog and using it as a 'stooge'. Work out how far away you are just before your dog responds in the way you're trying to address. This is your dog's threshold.

Now, repeat the same for yourself. How far away are you before you tense up or feel a little apprehensive about your dog's reaction? Your dog's threshold might be 20 metres, but your threshold might be 30 metres, at which point you're tense and tightening the lead. This helps you think about what signals you might inadvertently give to your dog. Without meaning to, you might be signalling to your dog to react.

Once you've established your thresholds, take the furthest one as your starting point. Be aware that you might need to give yourself a little bit more space as a buffer to begin with. Be aware of your hand movements and voice. Stay as calm and relaxed as possible, and avoid putting extra tension on the lead. You should signal that there's nothing to worry about. And remember, you're not yet going closer than the threshold, so you can relax.

Walk your dog towards the threshold,* remaining calm and relaxed, and as you get to it take a few steps backwards and recall your dog by saying 'come', or whatever your recall word is. If it follows your command, reward it.

A brief note on the reward type for this exercise. The idea is to keep your dog as calm and as unaroused as possible. Avoid using a toy that might excite your dog or build frustration. Instead, choose food. If your dog isn't that motivated by food, try doing this exercise before it eats, so that it's a bit hungry.

If your dog doesn't immediately turn and come when you call it, increase the distance between you and the trigger and try again. If it still doesn't come, then apply gentle pulsing pressure on the lead – don't pull or jerk it – aiming to get its attention, and encourage it to follow you. Reward the dog when it comes to you. Then, turn around and walk away from the trigger. You want to avoid getting the dog to the point where it begins to fixate and react. Remember, be mindful of the threshold so you set your dog up for success. Every time it reacts to the trigger, it fails, and essentially puts in another repetition to strengthen the habit you're trying to break.

Keep repeating this until your dog consistently shows interest in you, and gradually move closer to the trigger. Remember, you're

---

* It is good practice to walk with your dog on your left side. This will mean that when you walk with the flow of traffic, there will always be a safety barrier (i.e. yourself) between the dog and the moving traffic.

building a new habit here. You want your dog to move away from seeing the trigger as something to react to and instead see it as a reason to look at you, which then gets rewarded. This will take time, patience and, importantly, repetition.

This exercise helps to teach your dog to focus on you and leave everything else in the environment as background noise. It also helps to give you something to focus on, rather than responding in a way that signals to your dog to react to the trigger. It will keep your mind occupied and reduce the likelihood of you giving off smelly chemosignals that will set your dog off.

Keep repeating this and getting closer and closer to the trigger. You may hit a point where you feel you can't get any closer without losing your dog's focus on the trigger. At this point, get as close as you can to that threshold, and when your dog starts to fixate on the trigger, use a directional lead pop to snap the dog out of it and focus instead on you. This is like a firm tug of the lead towards you as you walk backwards. But remember, don't maintain tension in the lead. You're not trying to pull the dog towards you. Release the pressure as fast as you apply it. When your dog does look to you, reward it. The point is that it has already learned that the behaviour that betters its situation is to focus on you instead of the trigger, which is exactly what you want, too. It's a clear better choice for the dog.

If this doesn't work, don't give ever-harder lead pops. Some dogs might have strong genetic traits that are driving the behaviour. If this is the case you will need to work with a reputable trainer to establish any complicating factors and resolve the problem behaviour. The exercises here will have set you on the right path, a basis on which to build with a trainer. Many of the dogs that Danny works with haven't had the luxury of this foundational work, meaning the first few weeks of training are about building the basics. This will give you a head start and you will see more rapid improvement with a bespoke training programme tailored to your specific dog.

Now your dog has established the reward for the behaviour you want, it's time to strengthen its conditioning. Increase the distance between you and the trigger – if the dog's current threshold is 5 metres, say, go back 15 metres. Now, walk towards the trigger for a few steps and stop. If your dog stops and looks up at you, reward it. If it doesn't, overlay the message with a lead pop to get its attention, then take two or three steps and stop again. If it looks at you this time, reward it. If it doesn't, turn around, go back a few metres and repeat the exercise. We want the dog to learn that looking at you results in a reward, whereas failing to pay attention results in a lead pop and repeated exercise, which is less fun than a bit of cheese. Remember, the idea is that the lead pop should decrease the likelihood of the unwanted behaviour reoccurring; too many little pops can add to your dog's arousal by exciting it.

Keep repeating the exercise until the trigger is no longer a trigger. This might take days, weeks or months, depending on how triggered your dog is. But by doing this, we instil a new habit and retrain ourselves to respond in a way that doesn't contribute to a problem behaviour. Also keep in mind that you'll need to generalise this behaviour in a number of locations over time to make sure it is solid.

A final note. Every dog is different and it's important to always take a dog-centred approach to training. This exercise provides the foundations to counter-conditioning, but some dogs who are severely reactive to a trigger might need more techniques and exercises to effectively change their behaviour. In this case, explore your dog's needs with a trainer, but be assured that the principles in this exercise will have given you and your dog a great start.

Summary

- Dogs can pick up bad habits from each other by copying or using allelomimetic behaviours. Keep your dog separate from others who display problem behaviours until they are effectively resolved. If you bring an additional dog into your household, control the environment to prevent your existing dog from copying unwanted behaviours.

- Dogs also use social referencing to take their cue from us regarding how to respond to a situation. Actions like tightening the lead or changes in our voice when we anticipate their reaction can sometimes contribute to them seeing a situation as threatening and responding unhelpfully.

- Human sweat contains chemosignals that indicate mood. Dogs can smell human chemosignals and their behaviour changes accordingly.

- You can condition your dog to ignore environmental triggers and instead focus on you. Establish its threshold and reward it for paying attention to you. Gradually get closer and closer to the trigger, rewarding your dog for focusing on you and ignoring the trigger.

Chapter 4

What your dog is thinking
when you talk

Noah couldn't believe he'd caught it on video. He stood with his friends huddled around his phone's small screen at the bus stop, waiting for the bus to take them to town. The clip's star was Noah's family dog, a grey and white Husky called Dexter, apparently 'talking'.

'Look! Look! This is the bit,' he said eagerly.

The boys watched as the clip showed Dexter lying across Noah's legs on the sofa. Noah was stroking the fluffy grey fur across the top of Dexter's head. The dog closed his eyes, looking totally relaxed and content, and leaned into each stroke.

'Awwww, I love you, boy,' Noah said as he rubbed gently behind Dexter's pointy ear. At this point, Dexter opened his eyes and let out a mini howl that sounded uncannily like 'Yiiii ruv yoooooo', much to Noah's unbridled excitement.

'What's that? You love me?! You love me, don't you boy! Good boy, gooood boy!' Noah said as he fussed Dexter, chuckling to himself. Dexter was clearly enjoying it as he excitedly jumped up and started to play with Noah, nudging him with his head, wanting more scritches before pushing himself back into a play-bow. The video cut off with a view of the ceiling as Noah chucked his phone down to join in the game with his beloved Husky.

'See, I told you! I told you he said it!' Noah squealed excitedly.

'Oh, my days!' said Tom, one of Noah's friends.

'Play it again,' said another.

'You should put it on socials. I bet it would go viral,' said Tom.

'Do you reckon?' said Noah.

'Yeah, course it would! You should see some of the crap on there. I saw one yesterday of someone squeezing a spot that had two million views.'

Noah gagged slightly in response to the uncomfortable image . . . and then shrugged. Why not? he thought, so he opened the app and uploaded the video.

Dexter was a typical Husky. He had piercing blue eyes set in a white face that sat like a mask against his grey neck, head and ears. A thin rim of black surrounded his eyes, making him look a bit like a bandit. His fur was thick and springy. He was an energetic dog and followed Noah everywhere. Dexter was five years old, and Noah was fourteen. Dexter and Noah shared the closest bond out of everyone in the family home, primarily because Noah constantly interacted with the dog. They had pretty much grown up together, and it was obvious to anyone that they were best friends.

Huskies are extremely vocal. Whereas most dogs woof, with a blunt expulsion of air through their vocal cords, Dexter tended to almost pronounce every vocalisation. His woofs were more rounded, and he varied the tone like a mini howl. It almost sounded like words, but all merged into one. This was much to the entertainment of his human housemates, who would laugh and imitate his noises while fussing him, something Dexter found immensely rewarding – and which also served to reinforce the vocalisations. Dexter became even more expressive as he tried to elicit more attention from his humans.

Dexter wasn't speaking, although he was trying his best. But he was definitely communicating. At its most rudimentary, communication is exchanging information with another. That can be information about something, or an idea, even thoughts and emotions. Communication can happen in many ways. Between humans, it can be verbal or written. But communication can also occur without language, through non-verbal cues such as body language, expressions or gestures. Dexter scratching at the door and looking at Noah communicated his desire to go out to pee. Noah understood the message and opened the door. No words were exchanged, but intention and requirements were.

For communication to be effective, the sender needs to send a message that's clearly understood by the receiver. It's a fundamental building block to social interaction and crucial to building relationships; in this case, between dogs and humans. Given that dogs have been living with humans for tens of thousands of years, it's no surprise they have evolved to be good at communicating with us.

Domestication seems to have changed the way dogs communicate. While Huskies like Dexter are particularly talkative, dogs generally have a much broader vocal repertoire than many of their closest relatives. Let's take the wolf and the coyote. Wolves and domestic dogs shared a common ancestor twenty-five to fifty thousand years ago. Coyotes are part of the same genus as wolves and dogs, known as *Canis*. However, coyotes were never domesticated, so they have never been selectively bred for traits that humans desire. They are very different from dogs. They are pretty much nocturnal; they're sleeker than dogs and have a narrower chest and longer legs. Their ears don't flop like some breeds of dogs, and they have maintained their wild tendencies – such as being highly territorial and shy of people – in a way that domestic dogs have not.

Dogs vocalise in many more situations than wolves and coyotes.[1] Wolves and coyotes don't bark to greet each other, whereas dogs do. They don't vocalise to encourage another to play, whereas we often see dogs barking at each other to start a play fight or a game of chase. Dog's wilder cousins only tend to vocalise when defending themselves or as a warning.

Some scientists think that barking might have evolved as a result of dogs' relationship with humans. Wolves would roam over large

WHAT YOUR DOG IS THINKING

distances, so howling effectively communicated with other pack members who could be far away. On the other hand, dogs evolved living close to humans, making howling less necessary. It's possible that barking developed to make communication more effective between our two species over much shorter distances.

Noah was sure that Dexter barked to communicate with him. In addition to his newfound ability to speak 'English', which significantly enhances his cross-species communication skills, Noah recognised Dexter's play bark. It was usually a couple of short barks in quick succession, each preceded by a throaty growl. He had a different bark when stuck outside in the garden and he wanted to come in. It was more of a yip, yip, then a pause. It was almost like he was waiting for Noah to answer and say he was coming. When the doorbell went, it was a more rousing long bark – like a 'woowoow-oowoowoowoof'. As if he was shouting, 'Hey! There's someone here – quickly! Come quickly! Hey! Hey!' And when he was asking for food, it was more of a soft, winey, 'awoooo'. It was like he was begging Noah to give him a little scrap.

What do the barks say?

While it might be a stretch to describe Dexter's somewhat speech-like woofs as language, plenty of scientific evidence would suggest he is talking. Scientists in Budapest, Hungary, have used artificial intelligence to analyse more than six thousand barks recorded from dogs during different situations to see if there were any similarities.[2]

The aim was to see if specific contexts elicited similar kinds of barks, meaning the dogs were trying to communicate something about that situation. This would indicate that their barks had some meaning, like human words.

The researchers recorded fourteen Mudi (a type of Hungarian sheepdog) in six situations. This included a stranger appearing at their door at home without their owner being present; being involved in a fight (simulated with a trainer and a glove to bite on); preparing to go for a walk; being tied to a tree and the owner disappearing; a ball or toy being held in front of the dog; and finally a game being played between the dog and owner.

The recorded barks were fed into a computer programme which looked for similarities in barks in each context. The computer algorithm found that the barks could indeed be discriminated by context. They had acoustic features that depended on the situation. They meant something. The dogs were trying to communicate something about their motivational or emotional state triggered by that context. In the case of the person appearing at the door, it could have been to raise the alarm that there was an intruder. In the case of the game with their owner, it could have been the desire to interact through play. Either way, the dogs were trying to tell us something about the situation. And that something was being told similarly by all the dogs. The computer found they were all speaking the same language.

The other interesting finding was that the software could identify individual dogs by their bark. While many dog owners might not be surprised at this, given that we can often recognise our dogs by their voices, this is relevant because it was some of the first evidence that barks contain information about the *communicator's identity* to the listener. This is in addition to communicating how the dog might feel – whether angry, happy, playful or alarmed – and what it might want to do about it: whether it wants to attack or play, for instance.

Sometimes, we might misinterpret what our dogs are trying to tell us. When Dexter was a pup, he would spend much of his time in the house with Noah, his head and paws on the boy's lap, napping while Noah played computer games. When Dexter was relaxed, and the doorbell rang, he would raise his head, prick his ears, and let out a little, high-pitched bark, as if to say, 'Hey guys, what's that noise?' Noah thought the little woof was remarkably endearing. He would fuss Dexter and respond to his barks with, 'Who's that, boy? Is someone there? Is someone there for us, boy?', scratching his ears and play-pushing him as the dog jumped up and play-bowed, barking more.

Dexter's initial communication was to let Noah know that he'd heard something; it was a gentle alert bark in response to the doorbell. Then Noah 'rewarded' the behaviour of barking at the doorbell with praise and play. Before long, Dexter took the doorbell as a signal that he should bark, resulting in exciting fuss from Noah. Noah reinforced the behaviour and strengthened the link between that and the cue of the doorbell.

Very quickly, Dexter's small bark turned into a booming and excited bark, which soon tipped into a state of 'over-arousal' where he was so excited he could not control himself. He would bark, pant and jump around manically, unable to listen to anything Noah said because he was so worked up. He started to leap at the door every time there was a knock and even started smashing up the mail as the postie put it through the door. It got so bad the postman gave Noah's parents a warning because Dexter almost had his fingers as he pushed the mail through the letter box.

Although Noah might have got that communication slightly wrong and ended up with a problem he regretted, he was convinced that Dexter was better at understanding him. He was attuned to Noah's voice and the way he spoke. Once, when Dexter leapt up from Noah's lap to bark at the doorbell, his paw slammed down between Noah's legs and completely incapacitated him for several minutes. All the time, Dexter was barking, Noah was curled up in a ball with his hands protecting his delicate bits from further paw attacks, desperately trying to catch his breath.

By the time the pain subsided, Dexter had calmed down, too, and Noah was noticeably upset with his dog. 'Thanks a lot, boy,' he grumbled. Dexter turned and looked at him attentively. His ears went back, and he sidled up to Noah, his tail wagging nervously as he licked his face. He seemed to recognise the emotional change in Noah's voice and displayed 'appeasement' behaviours, which dogs use to try and placate others by being submissive, showing they are not a threat.

Do dogs process voices like we do?

Attila Andics and a group of scientists in the MTA-ELTE Comparative Ethology Research Group in Budapest, Hungary, were curious as to whether specific parts of a dog's brain are sensitive to human voices and whether human brains are also sensitive to dogs' vocalisations.[3] They set up an experiment where they scanned the brains of eleven dogs and twenty-two people while listening to sets of identical sounds. These included human voices, dog vocalisations, background noise with no voices, and, finally, silence (which gave the researchers a baseline where participants' brains weren't processing any noise). They were particularly interested in similarities in brain activity when each species was listening to vocalisations – whether human or dog – to see if there was anything special in comparison to other noises.

Incredibly, the scientists found the first evidence that dogs do have specific areas in their brains for processing the voices – something previously only seen in primates. But, remarkably, this applies to both dog and human vocalisations. The scans showed dog brains processed voices in a similar way to people. Both species had sound-sensitive brain regions in the *auditory cortex* and *subcortical regions* (where more primitive functions are processed, like emotions). It appears we use similar brain machinery and treat each other's vocalisations as voices rather than just any old sounds, which would suggest that they are a meaningful type of noise.

The researchers also manipulated the emotions of the human and dog vocalisations that were played. Some were emotionally positive, like happy voices. Others were negatively charged, like they were angry or sad. The scans showed that both dog and human brains seemed sensitive to emotionality, too. Dogs responded similarly to the emotional state of other dogs and humans. There was activity in the right central *ectosylvian gyrus*, a part of the brain close to the primary auditory cortex.

Humans showed a similar but weaker effect in the *bilateral rostral Sylvian gyrus* region for human – but not dog – vocalisations. This indicates that we need to up our game! It would appear dogs are more sensitive to the emotion in our voices than we are to theirs.

This matters in training – even if your dog doesn't understand all the words you use, you can be sure it's picking up on your mood. It uses your voice to read you. It matters less what you say and more how you say it. Be careful with your words. They're more powerful than you think.

Noah checked his phone to see whether his video of Dexter talking had gone viral. Much to his disappointment, it only had thirteen views. And Noah suspected that at least seven were from his nana, Doreen. She was always stalking his account.

While scrolling, he noticed a definite increase in funny dog videos that the algorithm was pushing his way. He found himself engrossed in videos of 'Mila The Talking Dog'. Mila, a sweet-looking Aussie, Collie and Husky mix, even has her own YouTube channel[4] showing her pressing buttons on the floor to talk to her human. She pressed a button that said 'scratches' and then 'Mila' and looked over at her owner expectantly, who dutifully came over, full of praise, and delivered her scratches right on cue. Noah was amazed. There were dozens of buttons, and Mila seemed to understand what each one represented and could combine them in a way that appeared to simulate speech.

Is it possible for dogs to understand what we say? Or could Mila have just formed associations between the sight of particular buttons and the things they represent, all facilitated through simple rewards when she got it right? We know that dogs are hyper-social with people, and there is evidence that they can recognise up to a thousand words to discriminate between objects.[5] We need to work out whether dogs can understand the meaning of words or whether they associate a word with an object that they've learned to pair it with through recognition.

Understanding language requires somewhat complex processing of both vocal sounds and their meaning. When listening to speech, human brains separately analyse the *lexical cues* (about the words) and the *intonational cues* (about how the words are said). Then, both sets of cues are combined to interpret the message. This might be the difference between hearing someone say, 'I'm really happy about that' in a bright and breezy way to indicate they are happy about something, or saying precisely the same sentence but through gritted teeth in a sarcastic way. The intonation here would suggest they are, in fact, far from happy. The same words can have completely different meanings when they're combined with the intonation.

Understanding speech takes so much processing power that humans have specific neural machinery to process language in the brain's left hemisphere. *Broca's area* is important for producing speech, and *Wernicke's area* is primarily involved in understanding language.

Several of the researchers involved in the previous study joined up with a few fresh faces to continue scanning the brains of dogs to see whether they process words similarly to humans.[6] We know dogs can respond to words in a way that suggests they understand what we want them to do, like 'sit' or 'lie down'. We also know that they listen to the emotional tone in our voices. But to what extent can they understand this? Is it as simple as 'sit', which means 'I sit and get a treat'? Or do we need to give them more credit for the way they process our speech?

The scientists put the dogs in the fMRI machine. They scanned their brains, giving them various combinations of praise or neutral words in either a praising or neutral intonation. The idea is that if dogs process words and their meanings, the brain's reward centre will be activated when they hear praise words spoken in a praising way. But if the dogs were only responding to the intonation – the way someone was speaking – then any neutral word said in a praising way should get the same effect.

They found that neutral words didn't fire up the reward circuitry in the same way. The dogs processed the words and how they were said separately, and then combined them to find meaning.

Like humans, dogs seem to have a particular place in their brains where they process words. Processing meaningful words – regardless of the intonation – occurs in the left middle *ectosylvian gyrus*. As with people, this is in the left side of the brain. The scientists also found an area for distinguishing the emotions in words, rather than the meaning of words (which was processed elsewhere).

When both the word and the way the word was said signalled praise, the researchers saw more activity in the brain's reward regions – the caudate regions. There seemed to be more activity connecting them and the auditory areas, suggesting the sounds the dogs were hearing made them feel good.

What's truly incredible is that dogs have specialised brain machinery that allows them to analyse word meaning and the way something is said separately, and then integrate them to derive meaning from them. This also tells us something about the evolution of language processing because this ability has evolved in dogs without them actually having language. It invites us to consider whether language skills, from a neural perspective, aren't unique to humans. The only edge that we have is the oral range to formulate words.

Noah was sure that Dexter understood more than most people thought. He was incredibly sensitive to Noah's words when he was speaking. Once, when playing Call of Duty with a group of friends, Noah was directing his teammate and said 'Turn left at the building and it's a bit further down'. When Dexter heard the word 'down' he lay down, looking expectantly at Noah, waiting for his reward. Despite the word being embedded in normal speech, Dexter was able to process it, identify it, extract meaning and duly obey what he thought were his human's wishes.

One crucial aspect of communication is 'intent'. The communicator 'intends' to convey a message to the listener specifically. With people, this can be as simple as using someone's name so they know the communication is meant for them, or by using eye contact or touching their arm. Even infants who can't yet talk are sensitive to communicative intent through eye contact and using names to signal attention.

Dogs are also incredibly attuned to humans' communicative intent; in some ways, even more so than other primates. Researchers conducting 'object choice studies', where dogs have to choose between objects, found that when humans pointed to a bucket, the dogs would make a human-like inference that there was food and search for it, something that not even great apes could do.[7] Their social intelligence across species is remarkable.

Gaze, point, talk – a recipe for good communication

You might be surprised at just how tuned in to our communication and social situations dogs are. A group of researchers from the Institute for Evolutionary Anthropology in Germany ran a series of experiments to investigate how dogs can tell when a communication is intended for them.[8] In the first of the experiments, they took twenty-six dogs and sat them in front of two cups, one containing a little bit of dry dog food.

The experimenter would either point 'intentionally' at the correct cup, while repeatedly looking at the dog and then the cup, or point 'non-intentionally' by stretching out their arm as if pointing at the cup but then checking their watch, while not making eye contact. The experimenter would also try an 'intentional gaze' where they would establish eye contact and then turn their head and look at the correct cup, as well as 'non-intentional gaze' where no eye contact would be made, but they would move their head to face the dog and then the cup repeatedly.

They found dogs were pretty good at identifying intentional communication. They went to the right cup when the human pointed intentionally, using gaze as well, but didn't do so when there was a more random, non-intentional pointing gesture. Similarly, dogs used gaze alone as an indicator of the right cup. Still, they didn't manage it without eye contact. The dogs seemed to use eye contact to indicate whether the human was trying to tell them something they should listen to.

A follow-up study with seventy-two dogs examined the importance of using the dog's name. An experimenter took one dog at a time and began with their back to the dog, and either called the dog's name, a random name, or called a random name while addressing another person. At the same time, the experimenter either pointed towards or gazed at the correct cup.

The dogs pretty much always followed the pointing, regardless of the name called. But when the person relied on gaze to communicate, the dog would respond when its name or a stranger's name was called. Still, interestingly, it didn't do so when the experimenter was addressing someone else. The dogs appeared to recognise the communication wasn't directed at them. Dogs don't just use eye contact to know that we're speaking to them. The fact that they responded to both their name and a stranger's name would suggest they're probably not reacting to the name specifically but to the high-pitched tone used to call. Or they assume communication is for them by default unless they see it directed elsewhere.

You might wonder whether the dogs have simply learned to respond to high-pitched calls, so they responded to both names. The study teased out the answer by repeating the experiment with puppies with very little previous interaction with people. The puppies responded similarly, suggesting it's less likely to be learned through interactions but more likely a more innate response to pitch. This might explain why Dexter got so excited about Noah's praise when he first reacted to someone at the door – he's hardwired to be attuned to high-pitched speech.

It's not just words that are important in dog–human communication; eye contact, pointing and tone of voice are all critical cues that dogs pick up on and digest to understand what we're saying. This is similar to human infants and suggests something more innate. It might be due to our closely bound evolution in social groups, including dogs and humans.

Try this: Teach your dog to 'speak'
If you want to capitalise on your dogs' communicative skills, you could teach them to bark on command. You'll later see that this can also be helpful as the foundation to teach your dog to stop barking as well.

Find something your dog loves, something that excites it. For some dogs, this might be food. For others, it might be a toy or a ball. Hold it in front of your dog: seeing it will make the dog want it. Then withhold the item. This will frustrate the dog, and should result in a vocalisation. To begin with, this doesn't have to be a full-on bark. It can be something minor, like a yip or even a sigh. Immediately reward your dog with food or a toy.

Do this a few times and gradually become more particular about the quality of the noise your dog makes before you reward it. While you initially rewarded just a noise, move to a place where you only reward a bark. Next, we will add a word to make them bark on cue. For this explanation, we'll use 'speak'. Say the word the moment before you anticipate the dog will vocalise, then reward it when it barks. Repeat this for a while, then, gradually, only reward when it barks twice. After a while, insist on three or four barks, and eventually insist on more consistent barking to get a reward.

Try this: Introducing quiet

Once you and your dog have mastered the 'speak' command, you can build on it by introducing a command for 'quiet'. First, get your dog to bark with your 'speak' command. Then say 'quiet', or your chosen command,* then move your dog's reward, clutching it to your chest to get its attention. Remember the concept of overshadowing from Chapter 2 – the sound should be followed by the action so that the action doesn't become the cue. You're looking for a slight pause in barking, which is then rewarded. Build this up gradually to reward your dog after longer and longer gaps. If it yips or barks, say 'ahah . . . quiet'. Then, reward it once it is silent. In this context, 'ahah' is used to distract your dog. To your dog, it may be an unusual sound it rarely hears. Using it should grab your dog's attention and it might give a split second of silence while it tries to compute it. Capitalise on this silence and reward it. Don't rush this part, or clarity will be lost.

Withholding something your dog finds rewarding is called 'negative punishment': you're holding back something it wants to decrease the likelihood of doing a behaviour. It's a bit like confiscating a teenager's phone because you caught them vaping, the intention being that it puts them off doing it again. After all, they really want their phone. In this case, you want your dog to stop barking when you give it the command, so you withhold the reward until it stops. Negative punishment is often

---

* Dr Sab teaches Luther in Hebrew, predominantly because she was fed up of other people in the household using different words and confusing him, so his 'quiet' command is *'sheket'*.

used in conjunction with positive reinforcement – giving your dog the reward when it does something you want it to repeat.

This exercise works best once you've built a solid 'speak' command where your dog will consistently bark. At that point, it understands the command and the expectation clearly, making it easier to work out what you need it to do for 'quiet'.

Try this: Stop your dog barking at the doorbell
Once you're confident that your dog clearly understands both 'speak' and 'quiet', you can introduce a trigger that sets your dog off barking, and then work together to stop this from happening. In this case, we'll use the doorbell.

Preparation is vital for this exercise. Make sure that you set up your environment so you can control it. You want to avoid someone ringing your doorbell when you are partway through, so make sure you're not expecting guests or a delivery.

Put your dog on a lead so you can stop it from running around and getting over-excited. Start close to the door so the door is a clear trigger. Ring your doorbell (ask someone to help you, or you can try using an app on your phone; you could even buy a cheap doorbell that sounds the same that you can hold in your hand and press). Immediately after it rings, and barking starts, say 'quiet'. Reward your dog when it gives you a moment of quiet again.

There's a good chance that your dog will bark when it hears the trigger because it's too aroused. In this case, wait for a break in the barking and reward that. If it is too aroused to listen, there's a good chance it's also too excited to take note of your reward. In this case, you could try an 'interrupter', like a pop on the lead. Then, repeat the command 'quiet' and reward it when it quietens down.

Once your dog has repeated this consistently, you can advance the exercise by taking it into the living room, or part of the house where it usually gets over-excited at the trigger. The context will serve as an additional cue to increase its arousal levels, making this exercise more challenging. Be patient and be consistent.

Once your dog has this down to a tee, you can take off the lead and continue rewarding it for responding to the quiet command when it's barking. Clarity is the most critical aspect of this exercise. Once it clearly understands, you can fine-tune this by ensuring that it responds solidly, even when something triggers it to be super-excited.

Dogs are like people in the sense that what works for one doesn't necessarily work for all. If your dog doesn't respond to a lead pop, there's a chance it could be over-aroused. This will be because the interrupter isn't sufficient to outweigh the level of arousal towards the door. If this is the case, don't give increasingly intense lead pops. Be careful going at it alone any further as this is a crucial stage that can lead to negative behavioural fall-out if you get it wrong. Rest assured: all your fundamentals are in place. Work with a reputable trainer who can help you put the cherry on the cake.

This exercise will be very difficult if you have more than one dog. As we have seen, dogs tend to emulate each other, and in this case barking will be contagious. If you want to do this in a multi-dog household, train each dog separately and entirely out of earshot of the other dog. Preferably, ask someone to take your other dog or dogs for a walk when you practise this exercise until it's completely solid. Then, repeat with the other dog or dogs. Only do this exercise with the dogs together once they can perform consistently individually. If their arousal levels are still too high, you'll be setting them up to fail.

Summary
- Communication requires a message to be sent by the sender and understood by the receiver. It can happen without language.
- Dogs have evolved to be sensitive to human communications and are adept at communicating with people.
- Dogs have specific parts of their brain that process human vocalisations, combining the words and the way they are said to derive meaning.
- Teach your dog to 'speak' by building frustration to make it bark and rewarding it. Gradually, start to reward only the clear barks, and then build it up until you only reward bouts of barking.
- Teach your dog 'quiet' by withholding its reward, marking when it is quiet, and rewarding its silence. Build the duration gradually so you only reward longer periods of quiet.
- Use these new commands to teach it to be quiet when the doorbell rings so that it learns a new behaviour to replace disruptive ones.

Chapter 5

What your dog is thinking about love

Molly was sauntering along a tree-lined path in the park, soaking up the midday sun. The hot weather was her favourite thing. She loved to feel the heat prickling her skin, reminding her of holidays past. Ernest, her adorable little Dachshund, was trotting along beside her. His legs were so short that his belly almost skimmed the ground, and his ears were disproportionately long for his head and face. Most 'sausage dogs' are black and tan, but Ernest was a liver-brown colour with orange eyebrows. He was odd-looking, but unquestionably cute.

Molly adored Ernest. He went everywhere with her, and she considered him her best friend. She wasn't really one for people. Instead, she preferred her own company or that of her dog. She enjoyed the closeness of her bond with Ernest, which came without the complications and uncertainty that too often surrounded human relationships. Ernest seemed to love her unconditionally, and she felt that her heart was almost bursting with love for him in return.

She was never happier than when she was walking in the sunshine, and she wanted Ernest to experience that joy. She thought he would love an amble through the park to a little café that sold dog-friendly ice cream made from goat's milk. She'd mistakenly given him a Mr Whippy once, not foreseeing the lactose-induced diarrhoea that later ensued.

Molly looked down at Ernest as they wandered along the path. He looked up at her with his tongue hanging out, whining gently. He would often whine to be picked up, which Molly believed was his way of reciprocating her love. She noticed he was picking up his paws quite high, and she smiled to herself, thinking he must be happy because he was prancing. In reality, the pavement was too hot for his paws and he whined because he was overheating. Dogs take about thirty days to acclimatise to a change in temperature. So, on the odd hot day we get in the UK, where we all flock outside to enjoy the sunshine, that's the day that's most likely to kill your dog. At such times it's best to walk your dog in the morning or the evening when it's cooler.

Things we enjoy – like sunshine and ice cream – aren't always so enthusiastically appreciated by our furry companions. Dogs, unlike humans, can't sweat, making them highly vulnerable to overheating, which can escalate into life-threatening conditions like heat stroke. Molly wanted to share an experience that would make her dog feel good. In doing so, she inadvertently anthropomorphised or attributed human traits and characteristics to him. Although we love our dogs, we do them a disservice if we miss out on how to love them as dogs, not as other people. That doesn't mean we love them any less. Rather, we think more deeply about what dogs need, instead of what people like.

Molly hadn't ever really thought about this. She loved Ernest so much and wanted to show him the same affection she knew would make her feel loved. She thought love was all he needed. Molly had always considered herself a little quirky. She dressed in a way that made her happy rather than fashionable. She wore baggy jeans and small T-shirts all year round. The only difference was that, in summer, she swapped her trainers for flip-flops. She was happy being single. She had her own home and valued her independence . . . and most importantly, she had Ernest.

Ernest was, without doubt, her closest relationship. She was a freelance writer, so she predominantly worked from home. Sometimes, when she felt like a change of scenery, she would go and work from the café in the village. Of course, it was dog-friendly, so Ernest went with her.

He would sit on her lap while she had dinner and cuddle next to her when she was relaxing on the sofa in the evening. And at night, rather than sleeping on his deluxe fluffy dog bed embroidered with his name, he would sleep in bed with Molly. She would often snuggle him just like a child would a teddy. His long body made for perfect spooning. By her own admission, she was obsessed with him. Not content with having his picture as her wallpaper and lock screen, she even had his face printed on her phone case, too.

Seeing your dog as one of your closest relationships is not unusual. Many of you will know a 'Molly' – you might even be her! Lawrence Kurdek of Wright State University in Ohio decided to study the relationships between people and their dogs. He wanted to know whether we are as close to them as the people in our lives.[1] He was interested in this from the attachment theory perspective, which concerns the emotional bonds between people that underpin the style of relationships they are inclined to form.

For instance, some have a securely attached style, where they feel safe and stable in relationships. People with an *anxious attachment style* often crave closeness and fear being abandoned. As a result, they can be quite clingy or dependent. Others with an *avoidant style* prioritise their independence and avoid getting close, finding it hard to form deep bonds. Whereas others, with a more *disorganised attachment style*, have a mix of anxious and avoidant behaviours, leading to unstable and unpredictable relationships.

Putting the relationship style aside for a moment, Kurdek was interested in how people saw their dogs as figures of attachment, compared to humans. He asked nearly a thousand people questions about their relationships with the people who meant the most to them, and about their relationships with their dogs. He wanted to understand how close people felt to their dogs and how that compared to the way they felt about the people in their lives.

The results showed that people enjoyed their dogs' company and, as with human connections, they missed them when they weren't there. Both are important core features of feeling attached in a relationship. Some were incredibly close to their dogs and listed them in their top two closest relationships. Molly would definitely have done the same!

Those who felt attached to their dogs felt as close to them as they did to their mothers, siblings, partners and best friends. But – and sorry, dads – they felt even closer to their dogs than they did to their fathers!

The study also looked at the personalities of dogs and people. They found that when owners had high levels of 'openness' and dogs had high energy levels and intelligence, they seemed to forge a particularly tight-knit bond. People who score highly on the openness personality trait scale tend to experience a wide range of emotions very acutely – they tend to be empaths. They are good at recognising how others feel. It might not be surprising that they form strong bonds with their dogs and can likely recognise and relate to their feelings. Empathy is the basis for their relationships.

Molly could relate to this. She was always thinking about what Ernest might be feeling. But because she tended to anthropomorphise – or humanise – him, she didn't always get it right. Hence, she took him for a walk in the searing heat to get an ice cream because she thought he would enjoy it like she did, rather than keeping him somewhere cool until the temperature dropped enough for him to tolerate a walk comfortably.

Molly was a pretty open person. She felt big emotions for Ernest. Their relationship seemed more intense than a friendship; she saw Ernest as family and, more specifically, as her pseudo-child.

To be fair to Molly, many of us talk about our dogs like they're our children. We commonly talk about our 'fur babies' (or 'furless babies', in Dr Sab's case), and we talk about being our dogs' mums or dads. 'Alloparenting', or taking in an animal and caring for it as a child, is a common practice amongst humans across cultures, with some researchers suggesting it comes from an evolutionary need for humans to domesticate.[2] When we bring dogs into our homes, we welcome them as part of the family. We do so based on the knowledge we will provide a nurturing relationship. We give food, shelter, enrichment, education and company – everything, in many respects, that we would expect to provide for a child. So, is there any merit in looking at our dogs as a familial dependant?

A team of researchers from Massachusetts General Hospital joined with scientists at Harvard to test this. They ran a study in which they scanned mothers' brains when they looked at pictures of their children and at pictures of their dogs to see whether there were any similarities in neuronal activity.[3]

They concluded that the concept of a 'fur baby' might have more merit than we first thought. When the mothers were in the scanner, the researchers saw similar brain activity when viewing images of their children or their dogs. The brain networks involved in feelings of reward, emotions and bonding were all active. They also flashed pictures of someone else's child and dog, and neither elicited the same activity. Brain activity triggered by images of their dogs and children was specific to their bond.

Curiously, one part of the brain that lit up when the mothers looked at images of both their children and dogs was the amygdala. In previous chapters, we've looked at this small, almond-shaped nugget near the base of the brain that processes certain emotions, especially fear. This part of the brain is also important for bonding. In this case, the amygdala signals that something is emotionally important, leading us to focus on it and forming a bond. It's likely causing mothers to direct their attention to the needs of both the child and the dog in an emotionally similar way.

The comparable attachment bonds between human caregivers and their dogs or children makes sense. These bonds protect the child and the dog by maintaining proximity to their parent. It keeps them safe. Domestic dogs are heavily dependent on human care. They have evolved features that are geared towards engaging the human caregiving system. For instance, they've evolved eyes that are rounder than those of wolves and are more like those of human babies, encouraging us to find them cute and respond to them like infants. They became less anxious around people and more playful, again eliciting our attention and allowing us to get closer to and subsequently care for them.

The benefit to dogs is clear – they get looked after. But what do people get out of it? The study found that the benefit is partly the feel-good factor of that bond. The scans showed that the more attached mothers were to their dogs, the more areas associated with 'pleasantness' activated in the brain when they looked at the pictures of them. They expressed similar ratings of excitement and pleasantness when they looked at both their children and dogs.

But of course, while we love our dogs, they're not actually our babies – even in the case of Molly and Ernest. Some differences might give us a glimpse of the evolutionary underpinnings of these relationships. The study found more activity in the *fusiform gyrus* when mothers looked at their dogs. This region is important for processing facial and social information. Since dogs can't talk, we rely on insights from their facial expressions to interpret how they might be feeling and how we should respond. There's more activity because we're working that brain region harder with our dogs than with our kids.

Not unlike children, dogs thrive when they have structure and boundaries. Sometimes, when we only focus on loving our dogs, we miss out on giving them the understanding they need to succeed in a human home. Molly was guilty of this. Ernest had the run of the house. She loved him so much that she was forever throwing him tasty treats just for being there – not that it helped his waistline. He was grossly overweight for a small dog, and that made it harder for him to move around quickly without tiring.

Nowhere in Molly's house was off-limits for Ernest. He would go from room to room as he pleased, sit on the furniture without waiting for an invitation, and chomp chair legs like they were dental chews. He treated every household item like it was a personal toy. He would bark when he heard something, when he wanted something, when he was excited or at anything that moved on the TV screen. In fact, he pretty much always barked.

Molly was trying to make Ernest feel at home, but the message Earnest got was that he could do whatever he wanted, regardless of the consequences, resulting in problematic behaviour. The worst, perhaps, was his tendency to pee and poo wherever he pleased, whenever he pleased. Commonly, on Molly's bed! He would whimper to be picked up, and when Molly was busy and couldn't, he would vocalise profusely until he got his way.

Ernest's poor behaviour was a direct result of too much freedom and insufficient structure before being taught how he should live in the house, with clear rules and boundaries. He didn't realise his behaviour was bad. He didn't know he was breaking any rules because Molly hadn't taught him any. Like a child who's never been told 'no', Ernest was well loved but spoiled to the point of being a bit of a brat. In truth, Ernest was out of control. He only got away with it – just about – because he was small and cute and could be easily picked up and moved away. It might have been a different story if he was a 50-kilogram Rottweiler.

While there's nothing wrong with loving your dog as much as you love a child, it's important to consider what they need in relation to their species. It's too easy to see them as little people, and assume they can rationalise and understand the world as little people. But they need us to think ahead for them, ensure they have the structure they need, and give them the chance to express themselves as dogs. Even a child would expect to be told 'no', but, too often, we allow our dogs to get away with things until we reach the end of our tether. This isn't fair on our dogs, who then can't understand our unexpected meltdown.

Molly's brain is geared up to see Ernest as her fur baby – but what about Ernest? What's happening in his brain when he looks back at Molly? Research has shown that dogs are particularly attuned to human faces. But is Ernest's brain hard-wired for attachment as well as Molly's? Or does he look at her and just think about the treats she gives him?

A study by researchers at the Clever Dog Lab in Vienna set out to understand more.[4] They took a group of dogs and scanned their brains while looking at videos of three people. One was each dog's owner, the other was someone the dog knew but wasn't bonded with, and the third was a stranger. The point was that if the dogs were genuinely attached to their humans, they would exhibit different brain activity when they saw their owner than when they looked at a person they just knew.

In these videos, the faces of the people featured showed either happiness or anger. This helped the scientists unpick whether emotion made any difference to each dog's activity. They figured that if a dog was attached to its owner, even an angry face would trigger the parts of its brain involved in attachment. On the other hand, if the dog just linked their person with the provision of food, the angry face might be seen as a threat and therefore would get more attention from the fear regions of the brain than the reward regions (which are triggered by the happy face).

When the dog looked at its owner, there was more activity in brain networks linked with attachment and emotions, like the *bilateral insula* and the *rostral dorsal cingulate gyrus*. Parts of the cingulate gyrus were activated more, regardless of whether the latter looked happy or angry. This only happened with the person with whom the dog had a bond. This was an important finding because this brain area is involved with mother–infant attachment processes. When parts of the cingulate gyrus are damaged in animal mothers, they struggle to bond with their offspring and don't display the expected mothering behaviours.

There is definite attachment-like brain activity when dogs look at their owners, but it's also important to recognise that dogs are different from people. They're not as cognitively developed as humans; a dog's cognitive capacity is akin to that of a two- to three-year-old child. They can't reason in the same way we do, so it would be unfair to assume they experience love for us in the same way we do for them, even though brain activity shows remarkable overlap between both species. While it might be a more rudimentary form of love, it's no less special.

Molly instinctively knew that Ernest loved her, too. She could tell by the way he gazed at her while she stroked his belly when they were cuddled on the sofa, bingeing on Netflix shows.

Ernest loved being around Molly. He followed her everywhere, even to the toilet. Rolling her eyes, she joked that he was like her Velcro dog, but secretly she loved it. Until, that is, she needed to leave Ernest somewhere, and she couldn't go without him getting really upset. What she thought was him *wanting* to be in her company was him *needing* to be in her company. Ernest had *separation anxiety*. From a dog's perspective, that's a very different place. It's not, 'I like being near you', it's more, 'I can't cope being away from you. Please don't leave me, *ever*.'

Nevertheless, she loved the connection and the mutual need that she felt with Ernest. It was fulfilling, wholesome and – most of all – safe. She knew Ernest wouldn't hurt her or let her down like other people did all too often. And she felt a deep sense of satisfaction with the security that knowledge brought to their relationship.

The problem with love is that it's all too often blind. In Molly's case, she loved Ernest so much that she readily excused poor behaviour that could land him in serious trouble in other settings, like his tendency to growl if anyone came near her. She felt he was being protective, making her feel special. But in fact, Ernest was *resource guarding* her. He wasn't interested in her safety; he just didn't want to share her. He was basically saying to anyone who came close that Molly was his. He owned her and had exclusive access to her company and all the food and good things she provided. This is not a sign of a healthy relationship between dog and human, despite the unquestionable love flowing both ways.

Unfortunately, Molly didn't deal with it because she quite liked it. Instead of resolving the behaviour with Ernest, she would tell the other person to stay away. In Ernest's mind, growling was a strategy that worked – it got rid of the competition, and he could keep Molly and the comfort she brought all to himself.

This was bad on many levels. For starters, if Ernest was to bite someone, he could be seized and destroyed. The sad reality is that it would be Molly's fault entirely for not dealing with the problem sooner to protect Ernest. And by letting him practise the behaviour regularly, there is a good chance Ernest could get used to the feel-good experience that seeing off a stranger brings. The very act of resource guarding itself could become self-rewarding, making it even more difficult to break the habit further down the line. Whilst we might instinctively be happy that our dogs feel good, they're less able than us to rationalise and emotionally regulate themselves. Ernest's big feelings for Molly could land him in deep water, taking Molly down with him.

*   *   *

Despite his poor behaviour, it was clear that Ernest loved Molly back – even if he displayed it in somewhat unhelpful ways. The attachment-based activity we see in dogs' brains isn't just something they learn from us. It's a deep bond driven by their brain chemistry. They're quite literally built to trigger our love and to love us back. One important neuropeptide that's fundamental to this is oxytocin. It's a chemical that drives feelings of love, social bonding and trust in humans. It also underpins mother–infant connections, triggering affectionate behaviours from mothers that cement the bonds with their babies.

Many experiments have found that oxytocin levels increase in humans and dogs when they touch each other, or gaze into each other's eyes.[5] Being loved boosts oxytocin and makes us want to show more loving behaviours, which triggers even more oxytocin. We end up with a bio-behavioural loop that makes us feel good and keeps the love flowing.

It turns out that oxytocin may have been the critical factor in the domestication of dogs and the main reason we seem to have such a mutual bond despite being from different species. One remarkable scientist studied the biological changes that happen over time when an animal is domesticated. Dmitri Belyaev was a twentieth-century Russian geneticist who believed that animals become domesticated through natural selection based on friendliness. He spent six decades breeding silver foxes, systematically selecting the tamest and least aggressive to pair up and breed cubs from.[6]

Over the years, he noticed changes in the foxes' features similar to those seen in dogs through domestication. Their ears got floppier, their tails got curly, their fur changed colour, and they were much more relaxed than wild foxes. But the changes to their brain chemistry were by far the most telling. Belyaev found significantly less cortisol – the stress hormone – in the selectively bred foxes, as well as higher serotonin levels. Both are linked with reduced aggression.

Oxytocin has an important influence on the way serotonin functions within the brain. It triggers a release in those brain regions that process emotion, such as the limbic system. It also increases the receptors that are available to bind with serotonin, which helps regulate mood and behaviour. With more receptors, serotonin can more effectively balance emotions, leading to greater impulse control and less aggression. Essentially, serotonin helps calm the brain, reducing tendencies toward aggression and lowering stress. That's likely why Belyaev saw such a dramatic cortisol reduction in the foxes. Think of this as the difference between someone cutting you up on the motorway, causing you to gesticulate in a rage (with little serotonin and lots of cortisol), versus tutting to yourself quietly and getting on with your day (with lots of serotonin and less cortisol).

Similar differences in brain chemistry and behaviours have been found in comparisons between wild and domesticated rats,[7] suggesting there is something about this trait that is important in order for animals to develop a connection with humans. We can see these traits in different breeds of dogs in modern days, too. Dogs that are more 'primitive', like Dr Sab's Xolos, have not been selectively bred by humans for specific traits and retain many of their wild tendencies. They're more likely to be reactive and nervous of new people than Danny's Labrador, Flint, for example. Labradors have been bred for traits such as docility and retrieving, which is why they make such good gun dogs. They fetch well and most are easily trainable.

The intricacy of biology is so profound that studies have found links back to dogs' genetic map that drives them to seek out the kind of interactions with people that bind us together. One study found a specific gene that made dogs more likely to direct their gaze towards people, resulting in the release of oxytocin, which drives social bonding and a sense of love and which underlies those docile traits that are so important for thriving through domestication.[8]

Variations in the gene DRD4, linked with dopamine receptors, social impulsivity and aggression, affect how long dogs look to their owners for help in an 'unsolvable task'. Researchers looking into this put some food in a container that dogs couldn't open without human help. They found differences in this gene, linked to how long the dogs gazed towards their owners. Dogs with the shortest allele (a different version of the same gene) looked towards their owners more and were more dependent on them. This was clear evidence that dogs are wired to bond with people at a genetic level. And the variation between dogs might also explain why some seem to like people more than others.

Dogs aren't just substitutes for human relationships or for children. They provide a sense of consistent relationship security in a way that people don't. Being with your dog is uncomplicated and feels good. It's secure. People can be much more demanding. We know that dogs change their brain chemistry to bond with us, and we do the same. This is mind-blowing when you consider that it occurs across two different species to form a sense of 'love'. But with that knowledge comes the responsibility that we need to guide our dogs, just as we do with our children, ensuring they know the rules and have the structure they need to help them thrive in a human environment. There is something important about giving your dog what it needs, not just what you think you'd want if you were a dog. Loving them isn't enough on its own. If you love your dog, train your dog.

Try this: Creating structure to help your dog thrive
As we saw with Ernest, giving dogs too much freedom before they've learnt the ground rules can allow them to practise behaviours you wish they didn't, like chewing on furniture or peeing on the bed. The best approach is to prevent this from happening in the first place by establishing some structure and

a routine with clear boundaries. The good news is that it's never too late to do this. You could start today and drastically improve your dog's behaviour, leading to a happier dog and a happier human.

In Chapter 1, we discussed crate training and the power of providing a safe space where your dog can switch off. The crate is our starting place for introducing structure, and this exercise assumes you have already crate-trained your dog.

Whenever you are not actively engaged with your dog, place it in the crate to allow it to decompress rather than giving it the run of the house. Don't worry, this won't be forever, just while we establish some new boundaries that will help your dog. Remember that the crate should be large enough for it to stand up and move around in comfortably, but not big enough to pace around.

The idea is that the crate should be boring and unstimulating, thereby encouraging your dog to switch off. Don't leave any toys or bones in there as the dog won't learn to relax. It's the equivalent of being in a quiet, peaceful bedroom with the TV turned off and your phone put away to help you to get to sleep. Your dog can have those toys or bones later for something to enjoy, just not while you're building new habits.

Initially, take the dog out of the crate regularly and do something with it – even if only briefly – then put it back in to decompress. This might be to pop into the garden for the toilet or go for a walk, even a bit of play time with a toy or practising some commands. Every time, give your dog the chance to decompress immediately afterwards by putting it back in the crate.

We want our dogs to learn that being inside isn't the place to be aroused and excited; it's the place to be calm and follow the ground rules. This also helps prevent separation anxiety. Some dogs used to being amongst the action might whine a little bit. It's important to ignore them, as you don't want them to learn that nagging will be a successful strategy to get their own way.

Always pop a lead on when you take your dog out of the crate, bearing in mind this will only be needed in the short term. Don't interact with or fuss the dog. Being inside the house should be boring, like it is in the crate. If you play, you get it excited, and this can make it frustrated when it's in the crate because it wants to get back out and join in the fun. Remember, this is about teaching your dog to relax in the house.

If one of the problems you're trying to solve is peeing or pooing in the house, take your dog out every two hours during the day to go to the toilet. Ensure it's on a lead every time, and as soon as it's gone to the toilet, give praise and reward, then take it back to the crate.

If your dog has an accident in the crate, don't worry. Don't scold it – it won't understand what it's for. Just clean up the mess and take the dog out more frequently until you're more familiar with its toilet habits. For example, you might take it out three times over six hours and it might only go the first and last time. Then you know roughly that six hours is the length of time it can go between toilet breaks (depending on how much it has eaten or drunk in between). The aim is to break the habit of toileting inside.

Feed your dog in the crate, too, as it's a great way to learn that good things happen in there. Prepare the food while the dog is in the crate, and bring it out on a lead. Tell it to sit, and once it is doing so calmly, put the food in the crate, then pop it back in to eat it. The dog mustn't be left with any uneaten food, because if it is genetically predisposed to resource guarding* (where it can become aggressive if you try to take food away), this might trigger it. Give your dog a few minutes to eat, and once it's had its fill, remove the bowl and any uneaten food. This is particularly important with rescue dogs, where you don't know their history and so should always err on the side of caution.

It's time to implement a structured routine after doing this for roughly four to six days, or once your dog has demonstrated that it can settle and switch off in the crate (some might be ready sooner, some might need longer). Give it crate time, then take it out to do something – like a couple of minutes of obedience training – then put it back in the crate. Leave it a while, then take it for a walk, but then return and put it back in the crate. Bring it out again on a lead and let it settle by your feet while you watch TV so that it gets some chill time in the house, then pop it back in the crate. Every time you take the dog out to do something, you can start to combine it with a toilet stop, then let it chill by your feet in the house again. This isn't an overnight fix. We're looking to build a habit.

It's important to give your dog crate time when there is activity in the house and people are around, not just when you go to bed and the house is quiet. This will help your dog to understand that it doesn't have automatic access to people and fun. When it understands this, it won't get so over-excited in the house and will be able to switch off much more easily. This is such a powerful way of reducing the chances of your dog

---

* Some dogs are naturally inclined to resource guard, and some grow to enjoy the act of resource guarding itself. If you experience this with your dog, work with a reputable trainer who can tailor a personal training plan.

experiencing separation anxiety. Your dog feels happy, safe and content in its own company.

Once your dog can readily switch off in the house, you can gradually increase its freedom. It can spend more time out of the crate, and you can interact with it more around the house. You can even go back to snuggling on the sofa – provided it only comes up when invited. Some people keep a crate in the house permanently; others prefer replacing it with a dog bed. Either is fine, so long as it works for you and your dog.

Try this: Preventing resource guarding
Resource guarding is a form of aggressive behaviour where dogs guard something they think is valuable. Dogs can resource guard food, toys and even the space around them, leading them to growl, bark and even bite anyone or anything that they think is close enough to take their prize away. All dogs are capable of resource guarding: it's actually a normal behaviour. When you watch dogs together in a social group, without the power of speech, they will growl and raise their forms of aggression to communicate their intentions. Although it might be a natural behaviour, it's not compatible with living in a human household, and the best way to deal with it is to prevent it from happening in the first place.

Without wishing to be a fun sponge, don't leave toys out for your dog to play with whenever it feels like it. This encourages it to see toys as possessions and gives it a chance to practise guarding behaviour, which is inherently self-rewarding. Instead, use toys to play and interact with your dog for bonding time, but then always put them away. This is a must-do and is particularly important for multi-dog households, where that tendency to guard could lead to a dog fight. It also strengthens your bond as your dog will see you as the bringer of fun.

When a dog guards an object, it can also start to claim the space around it. In some cases, the space claimed gets wider and wider, and in the worst cases, the dog will stop letting people into the room it's in with its object of value. Ernest claimed an armchair in Molly's living room, and neither she nor anyone else could go near it. Molly thought it was a bit like her dad, who claimed the comfiest chair for himself and would rebuke anyone else who sat in it. The difference was that Molly could have a conversation with her dad and negotiate an extension to her chair tenancy, whereas dogs don't have such powers of diplomacy. The only option they have is to elevate their aggression in the pursuit of a favourable result to better their situation.

A solid crate routine and structure will prevent your dog from laying claim to space around them. It also helps to train your dog to be invited onto the chair – or the bed – rather than jumping up and having free access to the space. Always start by doing this with your dog on a lead, and invite it up onto the chair with a command like 'up', encouraging it gently with the lead. Then reward the dog. Repeat this as many times as it takes for your dog to understand. Always combine this with a command to get down, like 'off', which you would teach in the same way.

If your dog is fed in the crate and they start to resource guard, work with a reputable trainer to tailor an approach for your specific dog.

Summary

- Some people see dogs as their closest attachment figures. It's possible to bond with a dog as strongly as you would with a human.
- The same brain patterns are seen when mothers look at both their children and their dogs, suggesting we are drawn to caring for our dogs as familial dependants.
- Dogs' brains show patterns of activity and chemical changes indicative of attachment to humans, suggesting the bond is reciprocated. There is evidence that dogs are genetically predisposed to bond with people too.
- Expressing love for your dog in the same way you might for a human, for example by giving it unlimited freedoms, can be detrimental.
- Crate training can establish good habits within the household and prevent dogs from practising unwanted behaviours.
- Start by teaching your dog to switch off in the crate and decompress before gradually introducing more freedoms. The best way to address resource guarding is to prevent it from happening in the first place.
- Do not leave out toys, bones or anything your dog finds valuable and might be inclined to guard.

Chapter 6

What your dog is thinking
when it's stressed

Some people seem to find everything stressful. The smallest things, like ordering a coffee but getting a cup of tea, can put them into a tailspin. People who see the glass as half-empty and react to little annoyances with a disproportionately big response. They're undoubtedly nice people, but they can't deal with the daily irritations of life. And because of this, they seem always to be in a bad frame of mind. They're permanently on edge, their anxiety making them sensitive to the next thing that's going to come along and trigger them. It taints the lens through which they see the world as they become acutely attuned to things that will stress them out. They notice those things more because they're looking for them, and then they do indeed find them stressful. Thus, the cycle continues.

We all know a dog that is perpetually strung out by life, too. One that's always a little anxious and afraid of the world. Smithers was a bit like that. He was a very cute, very cuddlesome, two-year-old Cockapoo. He looked like a teddy bear, covered in golden curls that tumbled down either side of big, button-like eyes. He was the quintessential adorable little puppy dog. There was only one problem. He was a dog that was always on edge. And that turned him from a bag of fluff into a bag of nerves.

His owner, Mia, got Smithers when he was a puppy. He had always been a shy dog, preferring to be picked up and fussed by her than by other people. Mia just put it down to Smithers being a sensitive and affectionate dog. So she thought all she needed to do was give him some extra love and reassurance, and he would realise that the world wasn't so scary after all.

As noble as her intentions were, they didn't make any difference. What started off looking like a preference for people he knew revealed a more general nervousness about anything he wasn't familiar with. Whenever Mia took him out, it was like he was walking on pins. He would be interested in sniffing everything, checking it out to ensure it wasn't a threat. He would pull on the lead so hard to get a better sniff that his breathing sounded like an old man who'd smoked sixty a day since he was nine years old.

Mia was frustrated by him pulling on the lead and tried putting a harness on him. It said on the advert that it was a 'no-pull' harness, but Mia thought it made him pull more, just a little more comfortably, without sounding like he was being strangled.

A harness doesn't stop a dog from pulling. It just makes it more comfortable to pull. We use harnesses to bear weight effectively. Whether the world's strongest person is pulling a lorry or a Husky is pulling a sledge, the harness distributes the force more evenly across a larger area, allowing you to bear more weight with less discomfort. It can also trigger 'opposition reflex' where dogs will instinctively resist an opposing force by pulling against it. You pull back, they pull forward.

Once dogs get into the habit of pulling, many find the act enjoyable. They're often pulling towards something they want – be that a field they want to get to or something interesting they want to sniff – and it results in a positive outcome. The pulling gets linked to that reward and becomes part of the dog's joy, much to their owner's misery.

Smithers was super-alert and would jump at unexpected noises, such as a bird fluttering out of a bush or a car door closing. Every time he was scared of something – which was pretty much all the time – he would bark, run towards the scary thing, and then go back to Mia, panting. Then he would start to whine, jump up and place his front paws on Mia's legs, which became her cue to pick him up. She would stroke his head and shush him as he wriggled around in her arms. She could feel his little heart beating ten to the dozen and hated seeing him so wound up all the time. She felt guilty and wished she could do something to stop him from being so nervous, but she didn't know what. So she would settle for trying to soothe him instead, although it didn't seem to help at all.

Being this stressed all the time doesn't just lead to unhappiness. It can have a significant impact on a dog's health. Just as stress results in a physiological response in humans, similar processes affect dogs. In people, we know that high levels of cortisol from chronic stress are associated with issues like obesity, heart disease and problems with the immune system, all of which can impact quality of life as well as longevity.

Nancy Dreschel, a researcher from Pennsylvania State University, wanted to measure the impact of stress on the lifespan of pet dogs.[1] Anxious dogs find the world a scary place. That constant anxiety triggers a stress response in the body, increasing the levels of chemicals such as cortisol and adrenaline. These changes prepare the dog for escaping danger quickly (i.e. fight or flight). But when these chemicals are constantly produced through anxiety, it results in a state of chronic stress. We know from human studies that this has an adverse impact on health, and Dreschel wanted to know whether chronic stress affected dogs similarly.

She asked owners of dogs that had died within the last five years questions about them. She wanted to tease out information to find indicators that the dogs were experiencing stress. Sometimes, behaviours we might think are quirks, like being scared of the hoover or chasing a shadow, are signs of an anxious dog. And anxiety can cause stress.

It turned out that anxiety – and subsequent stress – had an enormous impact on dogs. Stressed dogs died younger. Dogs that were afraid of strangers – like Smithers – on average died half a year sooner than other dogs.

Anxiety and stress not only shortened dogs' lifespans, they also seriously affected the quality of the dogs' lives. Dogs that were seemingly afraid of random things, like unexpected noises, and dogs that didn't like to be away from their owners, had more skin problems than relaxed dogs. Similar effects have been found in people because stress affects the epidermal barrier's function, leaving you more open to infections. This affected Smithers, too. He seemed to have constantly itchy skin, despite regular flea treatment. When Mia took him to the vet, he was diagnosed with eczema, which affects stressed dogs as well as stressed people.

Conversely, the more 'well behaved' the owner reported the dog was, the longer it lived. This wasn't because badly behaved dogs were put down (Dreschel checked for this in the data). This is because behaviours that people thought were bad, like barking or lunging, were due to stress. These dogs were trying to create space between them and the thing making them anxious by scaring it away. It was more likely that 'well-behaved' dogs weren't reacting to being perpetually on edge, so they lived longer.

Dogs always find comfort in things they know and can predict. Anxious dogs are scared because they don't know what a certain trigger will do. They can't predict an outcome and want it to go away. But there was one thing Smithers could expect – and that was Mia's reaction. When he was scared, he knew that he could jump up to Mia, and she would pick him up. It was less the fuss that comforted him and more that he had an outcome he could predict.

To be fair to Mia, most people, when stressed, would find being comforted by someone helpful. It's unsurprising that she intuitively thought soothing Smithers would help settle him. Mia thought she was helping to calm him down, but she was actually contributing to the problem. Research has shown that owners who pet their dogs when stressed make the situation worse.[2] One study found that the more their owners comforted them, the more fear the dogs displayed and the longer the fear lasted. Comforting dogs in this scenario offers them an unhealthy coping strategy that traps them in the cycle of fear instead of helping them to overcome it.

We can all relate to the sense of comfort in the familiar. The 'mere exposure effect' is a human psychological phenomenon whereby we prefer familiar things. However, this can also be why we return to situations or even people we know are bad for us. It's a similar loop with Smithers. Fuss from Mia didn't teach him how to overcome stressful things, but it trapped him in a cycle of thinking scary things require fuss. And by not dealing with the fear, something that is momentarily anxiety-provoking can turn into stress that becomes chronic and lasting.

We know anxiety and stress can impact the body of a dog to the extent that it can shorten its life. But could there also be a physical effect on the brain?

There are indications that this is the case with people. Humans who suffer from anxiety disorders have different brain activity in areas that are heavily involved in responding to fear-inducing things, the kind of things you might feel anxious about. The blood flow in these regions differs from that in people who don't suffer from the same disorders. Because these brain regions are more active – constantly registering fear – they need more blood to provide the oxygen to keep them working.

A group of researchers from Ghent University in Belgium combined their specialities in veterinary science and human medical science to compare activity in anxious dogs' brains with what we know about anxious people's brains.[3] They used a brain scanning technique called *single photon emission computed tomography* (SPECT), which shows how blood flows through particular organs. A radioactive tracer is injected into the blood and shows up on the scan. Sensors pick up the energy emitted by the tracers as they move to make an image showing where the blood is flowing.

The scientists scanned the brains of eighteen dogs, all of which had been referred to vets specialising in behavioural problems for severe and pathological anxiety. In other words, harmless things triggered their fear, and their behaviours were so intense that they affected the dogs' quality of life and their relationships with their owners. Their scans were compared to another group of nine dogs who weren't generally anxious.

Like anxious humans, the anxious dogs had different blood flow to parts of their brains involved in fear responses. The amygdala was more active, which makes sense as it is the part of the brain that registers that something is scary. The same was found in the hypothalamus, which processes information about the context of something frightening. The prefrontal cortex had reduced blood flow, likely because parts of it are dense in receptors that stress hormones bind to. But the prefrontal cortex is the part of the brain that usually sends signals to the amygdala to tell it to quiet the alarm.

This explains why everything seems scary to anxious dogs. Their brain machinery is wired to misprocess what they experience in the world, quickly categorising it as frightening. They are incredibly attuned to anything that might be fear-inducing. Their brains work differently, and their brain chemistry changes too. They have different levels of serotonin and dopamine, which are involved in regulating mood and anxiety-related behaviours, from non-anxious dogs.[4]

The anxious behaviours Mia saw in Smithers on the outside were all supported by changes on the inside that made him more sensitive to stressful things. His brain was attuned to triggers. Not only did he notice them more, he also responded with even more vigour. Without any actual intervention to teach him how to cope with the triggers, he got caught in a brain–behaviour loop. His brain focused on scary things, and his brain chemistry drove a fear response. That experience got logged and strengthened the circuit, meaning he was even more likely to respond the same way next time.

When he was about a year old, he became particularly nervous around people. This isn't uncommon as it coincides with a young dog's natural development of fear responses, which can happen between six and fourteen months old. However, because Smithers was anxious about new situations, he stiffened up whenever someone new came near him. Then he would stare at them and lick his lips a couple of times. Mia thought this was a good sign, that he was tolerating the situation calmly. But it was actually Smithers trying to say he was uncomfortable with what was going on.

Smithers tried this for a while, but Mia kept letting strangers try to pet him. She felt uncomfortable saying no when someone just wanted to say hi. Still, her heart would sink because she knew he wouldn't respond with a wagging tail and excitement, like most other dogs she knew. Eventually, he snapped at a woman who had stopped Mia in the street to say hello to the cute puppy. It surprised Mia, but not half as much as it surprised the woman. Fortunately, Smithers didn't catch her with his teeth, but he did frighten her.

Mia was lucky. This technically would have been considered an offence under Section 3 of the Dangerous Dogs Act (1991). According to this legislation, a dog is regarded as dangerously out of control 'on *any occasion where it causes fear or apprehension to a person, that it may injure them*'. Smithers didn't have to bite the woman to break the law, although the offence would have been aggravated if he had done. Smithers ran the risk of being seized and destroyed, and Mia could have found herself facing a magistrate in court.

Mia thought his outburst of aggression came out of nowhere, but the truth is that it didn't. He had been trying to tell her for months that he was uncomfortable with those interactions, but she kept missing the signs.

Mia isn't on her own. It turns out most of us aren't that brilliant at spotting when our dogs are stressed. A survey of nearly twelve hundred dog owners found that only about half of them could correctly identify stress[5] in their dogs. People would generally get the obvious signs, like a dog trembling or whining. But very few could properly interpret the early signs of stress that were arguably much more subtle, like stiffening up or looking away, turning the head, or licking the nose. Note that body language should be read collectively – for example, your dog might just be licking its nose after a drink of water, but if it's repeatedly licking it while doing a number of these other things then it might be an indicator that it's uncomfortable.

Only one in five dog owners even appreciated that stress could have long-term consequences for the health of their dogs. There was even disagreement between the sexes, with men generally thinking their dogs experienced lower stress. In contrast, women thought their dogs were moderately stressed. What is clear is that we're not, in general, great at calibrating whether our dogs are stressed or not.

We often project a very human idea of what stress looks like on dogs in terms of definition and experience. When Mia felt stressed – usually by her mother ringing and passing judgement on every aspect of her life – she wouldn't dream of licking her nose. Instead, she might zone out a bit. She would feel frustrated and would usually respond with some passive-aggressive comment. None of which Smithers could do. Instead, he would initially turn his head away, then start to stiffen up, and his eyes would widen and fix on the person who was making him feel uneasy. It was a subtle but powerful warning because the next response would be to bite to try and make the person back away.

It's easy to miss common behaviours rooted in stress in our dogs because they're so far outside our own lived experience. And it's natural to compare what we see with what we've felt or done in the past. None of this seemed to help Smithers, though. Mia had been desperate to get away for a bit and booked a dog-friendly cottage holiday in Cornwall. By this point, Smither's anxiety-related behaviours were so bad that he spent the entire holiday in a crate in the cottage while Mia took some respite and explored. She was too embarrassed to take him out or risk another bite with a stranger. He didn't love being left alone, though, and a few times, Mia could hear him whining from the bottom of the path as she returned to the cottage.* If only Mia had prepared for this earlier – it typically takes four to eight weeks to teach dogs with separation anxiety to be content on their own.†

Some dogs suffer from a type of chronic stress through separation anxiety. They become overwhelmingly distressed whenever their owner is absent. Thankfully, Smithers wasn't quite as bad as this, but he was definitely uncomfortable. And given how quick Mia was to try and soothe him with extra affection rather than teach him healthy coping strategies, it was likely to get worse. It is also incredibly common, affecting nearly one in five dogs in the UK and USA. That kind of chronic anxiety affects more than just the dog's behaviour. It affects the way their brains work.

For instance, it influences something called *brain-derived neurotrophic factor* (BDNF), a protein important for the brain's hard wiring in both dogs and humans. It preserves brain cells and encourages new cells to grow and connect. These connections allow brain cells to

* In this situation, Mia should ignore Smithers when she first arrives back, without interacting or making a fuss until he settles down, so that he doesn't associate the behaviours of separation anxiety with achieving the outcome of fuss from her.
† For a dog with more severe separation anxiety, this might take much longer.

talk to each other, which is vital for everything we do. It influences a vast range of functions, from mood to sleep patterns. BDNF is particularly important for brain changes that allow us to remember and learn new things.

As BDNF is prevalent in parts of the brain that are heavily involved in regulating mood, emotion and thinking (like the limbic region and the prefrontal cortex), it is perhaps unsurprising that dogs experiencing chronic stress through issues like separation anxiety have lower levels of it than other dogs.[6] Although Smithers wasn't yet too bad with being left on his own, the stress caused by his constant anxiety would likely have the same effect.

Seeing Smithers so stressed all the time broke Mia's heart. She just wanted to do normal things with him, like walk him in the park without being dragged around. Mia was embarrassed when he barked at things, thinking people would judge her for not being able to control him properly. She found herself feeling down and obsessing about the issue. She wondered whether she was the problem, and whether he would be better off with someone else who knew more about dogs.

After a very long and tearful conversation with a friend about how bad she was feeling, she was persuaded to try a dog training class. Maybe it might give Smithers a bit more confidence. But that didn't work either. He struggled to learn new commands and spent the whole lesson pawing at Mia's legs for her to pick him up. Even when he was standing of his own accord, Mia would try to lure him into different positions to teach him to sit on command. Still, he didn't seem to understand or learn much at all. He wasn't interested in Mia's treats because he was too anxious to eat (cortisol suppresses appetite, so a stressed or aroused dog won't take food). This is perhaps not a surprise, given what we know about Smither's brain machinery. The very parts that are important for learning had shut down, so it's little wonder Smithers couldn't retain anything useful. He didn't have the confidence to be open to new things.

Imagine you really want to learn how to dance, but the idea of attending a class fills you with dread. You have no one to go with, but you pluck up the courage to go alone. You get there and walk in. Everyone else seems to be having a great time; they all know each other and chat like old friends. You turn up alone, unsure of what to do and feeling nervous.

The music starts and you try to take part. You're not really feeling it. Your stomach feels tight, your palms are sweaty and you can feel your heart racing as you try to hang at the back on your own, desperately trying to keep up with the moves but making lots of mistakes. By the end, you feel like your nerves have got the better of you and you've learned nothing. It's the same for Smithers. In this situation, classes can hinder your dog's progress because you haven't helped it get to where it's ready to learn. The environment is overwhelming and the dog's senses are flooded, which limits its ability to retain information.

Studies have found that the best way to help dogs get through situations that they find frightening is to counter-condition them. This involves giving them something nice after the occurrence of the scary thing – like giving them a tasty bit of food after they hear a firework going off. One study found that around 70 per cent of dog owners succeeded with this approach,[7] although this will only work if the dog isn't too stressed to take food. So, to do this, you need to start small, like a quiet firework noise followed by food, and then gradually increase the volume. The idea is that once a scary thing becomes a precursor to a good thing; you have taken the fear away and replaced it with the feeling that something nice is coming.

The next most successful route was to undertake relaxation training and give the dog somewhere to switch off, which was successful in 69 per cent of cases. An example of this is teaching your dog to feel comfortable in a crate and to make that their safe space. For instance, if your dog is afraid of fireworks, this could be a helpful strategy for dealing with bonfire night. Alternatively, desensitising the dog by repeatedly exposing it in a controlled way was found to help in about 55 per cent of cases. This can be done by playing the noise that the dog considers frightening while it is relaxed or eating, quietly at first, and then gradually turning it up over several sessions.

Other alternatives, such as exposing the dog to pheromones (chemical messengers you sweat out), giving them nutraceuticals (food supplements) or homoeopathic remedies (which are often no more than glorified water) or other herbal products, proved pretty unhelpful. Owners only reported success in around a third of cases. They didn't work any more often than you'd expect with a placebo, basically by chance.

There is hope for anxious pet dogs. They don't have to live in environments they find stressful. We can learn a lot from working dogs, such as those used by emergency services, for example police or search-and-rescue dogs. These dogs work alongside their handlers in extreme environments amongst scenes of absolute devastation. Working dogs were used to search for survivors at the scene of the 9/11 terror attack in New York in 2001. It was a scene so devastating that human responders found it overwhelmingly stressful, with an estimated one in five people directly involved developing PTSD.

Given the high-stress environment, people were tense and displayed signs of stress, evident in their voices, their expressions, even their chemosignals – to all of which dogs are highly sensitive. One study conducted medical surveillance of working dogs that were deployed to the scenes of the 9/11 and Pentagon terror attacks to search for survivors to see how environments that were stressful to humans might affect the dogs working in them.[8]

This study was also interested in the dogs' behaviours, to ascertain whether working for an extended period in stressful conditions induced anxiety in the dogs in a way that could affect their health. They looked at a range of biological indicators. They analysed the dogs' blood, and found no medical or behavioural evidence that deployed dogs developed any adverse effects related to the stressful working environment.

Dogs weren't affected in the same way as people. It's likely because these dogs are taught to search for people to get a reward – usually their favourite ball and a game with their handler. So, situations that most people would dread don't actually represent the same negativity in the minds of these dogs. They were taught to focus on something and therefore the stressors present just melted into the background.

When a dog is anxious, the research shows that the amygdala goes into high alert, actively seeking things to be afraid of. Fortunately, there are some simple ways that you can help your dog focus less on the surrounding environment and more on you, which will ease its anxiety.

The following exercises are based on the associative learning concept of *negative reinforcement*. This is a crucial way that all living beings learn, where we do something to avoid or stop something we don't like. For example, if we have hunger pangs, we eat to stop them. We get out of bed to make the noisy alarm stop. A person finally gets round to tackling their task list to stop their spouse complaining. It is commonly used in classrooms as a behaviour management strategy – if a child behaves well for the remainder of the class, they might have their detention dropped. It can feel just as rewarding as positive reinforcement, where a particular behaviour or action is rewarded with something nice.

The following exercises were the basis of the foundational work that Mia did with Smithers while working with Danny. They're based on the same principle as dogs working in disaster zones having a task to focus on, allowing everything else to fade into the background and not be overwhelming.

After just a few weeks of consistent work, Smithers improved greatly. He started to walk nicely to heel without pulling Mia everywhere and quickly stopped lunging and jumping up at her. The exercises helped Smithers, because his amygdala was always on high alert as he was anxious about everything around him. It taught him there's nothing to be afraid of because he learned to focus on Mia, letting everything else fade into the background. His fears weren't addressed directly. They were dealt with indirectly by providing something else that took priority over the environment: Danny made Mia that something.

Try this: Teach your dog to leave everything in the background and focus on you
This exercise will teach your dog to focus on you and ignore everything else in the environment, stopping that amygdala alarm from constantly ringing. It's a similar concept to the amazing search-and-rescue dogs we heard about earlier. These dogs are so focused on searching to win the prize of their ball that they ignore all the stresses and strains of the environment around them.

Before we get going, your dog must understand how to walk to heel. If yours already does, you have a head start. But here's a quick rundown of what to do for those that don't.

First, we will teach your dog to understand the concept of lead pressure and what it has to do to release that pressure. That's the negative reinforcement aspect.

This exercise works best with a slip lead, slip collar or even a martingale collar. All of these tighten in response to your dog pulling on a lead. The aim is to provide sufficient pressure so that your dog will want to stop pulling, and you'll teach it how to do that by walking to heel, which will prevent the pressure.

Make sure the collar or slip lead is fitted correctly. It should be high up on the dog's neck, sitting just behind their ears. Without saying anything, allow your dog to choose a direction in which to start walking and take up the slack of the lead while you remain standing still.

As the dog takes up the slack, shift your weight in the opposite direction so you're slightly amplifying the lead tension. Hold that position without yielding to the pressure in the lead. You're looking for your dog to move in the direction that alleviates the pressure.

Slowly, step in another direction and let the dog do the same. Keep repeating this so the dog learns that moving closer to you removes the pressure. We call this *yielding to the lead.* As you repeat this, gradually shorten the lead until you're doing the repetition with your dog in the heel position, with the right ear in line with the seam of the left leg of your trousers. Once your dog starts to understand this, as long as it doesn't excite it, you can use words of encouragement when your dog is actively choosing to walk in the right position.

Now that the dog understands lead pressure, it's time to teach it the rules of the game you expect it to follow. The rule will be to stay in line with you in the heel position – this is the task on which you want it to concentrate. Once it knows how to focus on the task, it'll stop noticing triggers, and the world won't seem so scary.

This time, stop suddenly when your dog is alongside or slightly behind you. As you stop, watch what your dog does. Does it suddenly stop, too? Or does it keep walking forward? Does it look up at you? If it stops with you and looks up at you, calmly praise it for choosing to pay attention to you by saying 'good' in a soothing tone. Anything too animated might excite your dog and get in the way of continuing the exercise, so keep it calm and encouraging.

This exercise helps your dog realise that the lead that binds you might suddenly become tight if it pushes ahead of you or drops behind. When it does this, apply pressure in the opposite direction until your dog chooses to switch off that pressure and moves to the heel position. It helps your dog to walk nicely on the lead, which should be loose, as it takes its direction from your position rather than the pressure of the lead.

Keeping up with you and having you close keeps the lead nice and loose, so your dog learns it makes sense to keep an eye and ear on you to know where you are and where you're going. Once this is solid, you can add the word 'heel' whenever you are about to set off on your left leg. Naming the command after your dog has learned it and it meets your expectation, the word becomes associated with that precise behaviour. It gives your dog clarity.

Once this is really well understood, you can start to introduce positive reinforcers like treats to reward your dog for walking in the correct heel position. Positive reinforcement increases the likelihood of a behaviour occurring and will strengthen the heel position your dog has learned. As we're focusing on negative reinforcement in this chapter, it's better to teach your dog to understand lead pressure before you start adding in the rewards. This helps you to be clear it really does understand it thoroughly before you add in another step.

There are many ways you can teach your dog how to walk to heel. Remember to always take a dog-centred approach, and if this particular approach isn't helping your dog learn, there are many others you can try.

Try this: Teach your dog not to lunge
Now that your dog understands the task, we will move to the next exercise. This will teach your dog to ignore specific

triggers that it would usually lunge at or pull towards when you're walking.

In Chapter 3, we talked about working on your dog's thresholds, i.e. how close we could get to something your dog is aware of before reacting to it. We will start this exercise near your dog's threshold for something it would lunge at – whether it's a dog, an object or a person. But instead of recalling your dog near its threshold to get a solid, well-proofed recall, we will 'proof' the behaviour of walking to heel and focusing on you.

Keep an eye on your dog as you get close to its threshold. When you notice it starting to fixate, stop as your left leg strikes the floor and your right leg meets it so you're standing with your feet together. If your dog follows suit and stops with you, that's brilliant and may well warrant a reward* (bear in mind that if the reward over-excites your dog, you might need to hold off and make do with a calm 'good' instead). Keep repeating that, edging ever closer to the trigger. If the dog doesn't follow you straight away because it's focused on the trigger instead of you, abruptly turn around and walk away from the trigger, maintaining the same pace. If the dog's attention remains on the trigger as you're walking in the other direction, the lead will naturally tighten, giving your dog a pressure-based cue to switch it off by getting by your side. If you're dog isn't too excited, you can positively reinforce this with a treat at this point. Then repeat the exercise, initially from a little further away, and build your dog up to moving closer.

Bear in mind that dogs are all individuals and have varying levels of resistance to certain methods of training. If the above

* A reward isn't strictly necessary here because the dog choosing to release the pressure is bettering its situation so it's naturally rewarding. Like choosing your favourite food at a buffet – you don't need an extra reward for choosing it, you did so because you like it so it inherently feels good.

doesn't work, you can try a lead pop instead. If that isn't effective because your dog is too aroused or reactive to the environment, you might have gone too far, too soon. Try going back a few steps, increasing the distance from the trigger, and try again. Or put your dog away and try again when it is calmer, as it might be too aroused for the rest of the session. If these exercises have been repeated and you are still struggling, work with a reputable trainer to develop a dog-centred bespoke programme for your dog.

Once your dog succeeds in this exercise, you can start to overlay positive reinforcement, too. Offer a high-value reward when your dog notices a trigger but actively disengages to pay attention to where you are and what you're doing, while remaining in the heel position.

Try this: Stop your dog from jumping up
This exercise is designed for dogs jumping up for fuss or attention as a coping strategy for anxiety.* Again, this exercise is based on negative reinforcement, so it works best with a collar that will tighten when your dog pulls, like a slip lead, slip collar or martingale collar. Set up a situation where your dog would likely jump up and put its paws on you. If your dog jumps up when someone approaches, for example, or when it's near another dog, ask a friend to help you as your 'stooge'. This allows you to control the environment to set your dog up for success.

Initially, make sure you use the least arousing triggers, and try it in the least exciting place as possible. If your dog jumps up in the park, start doing this at home first. You need your dog

---

* If your dog is jumping up to bite, work with a reputable trainer who has proven results in aggressive behaviour modification.

to have enough clarity of mind to learn the new things you will teach it. If it's too aroused, it won't listen or understand what you're asking it to do.

Introduce the trigger from a standing position (rather than when you're walking). When your dog attempts to jump up, hold the lead 90 degrees above its head without saying anything, while preventing its paws from touching you. The pressure on the lead should be vertical, not diagonal, which would trigger its opposition reflex. This bit is very important – as soon as you feel the dog's weight yield, release the tension in the lead and just say 'good' (no rewards yet).

You are teaching the dog that jumping up doesn't result in a cuddle any more. It results in lead pressure. And to release that pressure, all the dog has to do is put its paws back down on the ground. It will only learn that if it feels that release as soon as it goes to put its paws back down. You don't say anything, like 'no' or 'ah-ah', because the dog needs to link the behaviour and the release without any other cues confusing it.

Repeat this exercise a few times, walking away from the trigger and back again if necessary. If the dog continues to jump up, carry on doing the same thing. Make sure you're absorbing the tension into the lead without jerking the dog. The aim is to help it to understand when the pressure will start (when it jumps up) and how to turn it off (by getting down).

Once you think your dog has got the hang of this from a standing position and has stopped trying to jump up when the trigger is near, end the session. It's imperative to finish positively with your dog once the lesson outcome has been reached. Leave it for at least twenty minutes, go and have a cup of tea, and then come back and repeat the session to see how much of the lesson your dog has retained. If your dog seems to go back to square one, it might be too aroused, so try being further away from the trigger or in an even less arousing environment. Like people, some dogs learn more quickly than others, so be patient and consistent. Repeat this exercise every day for a week until you're sure your dog has a solid understanding before you try it in more arousing environments.

Once mastered, you can try this exercise with your dog on the move. Take it for a walk and find one of its triggers to jump up. Remember your thresholds and repeat the smooth vertical pressure on the lead every time your dog jumps up to prevent its paws from touching you. When you reach the point where you are near a trigger and your dog doesn't jump up, say 'good' in a calm and monotone way. The message you want your dog to receive is 'I like that, keep doing it', but without making it excited as that will increase the likelihood of it failing the exercise and jumping up.

At this stage, there is no need to use positive reinforcement like treats. Clarity is fundamental. Once you've continued to raise the level of arousal in more challenging contexts and you're satisfied that your dog is choosing not to jump up when it normally would, you can add positive reinforcement within each type of environment.

When your dog sees a trigger and chooses not to jump up, give it a treat to reward it for making the right choice. Again, avoid toys that increase its arousal. The reward should always be because your dog has actively chosen not to jump up. Take care not to randomly provide rewards without it being clear what you're rewarding your dog for.

Summary

- Stress can shorten a dog's lifespan.
- Stress affects a dog's behaviour and sometimes causes the dog to display unwanted behaviours that impact on its quality of life and relationship with its owner.
- Stress-related behaviours are often subtle and easily missed by many owners.
- Stress affects how a dog's brain works, making it more attuned to environmental stressors and making it harder to remember and learn new things.
- You can teach your dog to ignore the environment and focus instead on you, like working dogs at a disaster scene. This focus on a task makes stressors less relevant and eases anxiety.
- First, teach your dog to understand lead pressure and walk to heel. Then, teach it the correct heel position with its right ear in line with the seam of the left leg of your trousers.
- Teach your dog not to lunge by keeping it focused on walking to heel and gradually practising this near a trigger, getting closer and closer to its threshold.
- Teach your dog to stop jumping up by teaching it that it results in lead pressure, which it can relieve by putting its paws back down. Once your dog solidly understands the concept, practise near a trigger, getting closer and closer to its threshold.

Chapter 7

What your dog is thinking about food – and its mood

'When we are considering how a dog is behaving, we really should be considering what is inside the stomach.'[1] This was a statement made by leading animal psychologist R. A. Mugford in an article on the influence of canine nutrition on behaviour back in 1987. It was a point made well ahead of its time and long before neuroscience had begun to uncover how closely connected the belly is to the brain.

We've all heard the saying, 'You are what you eat', and there's some tangible truth in that – for us and our dogs. Foods are consumed and then transformed into the building blocks of the body. Once food is digested and broken down into its constituent parts – lipids (fats), carbohydrates, proteins and other nutrients – it is absorbed through the intestines. From there, the body uses it to build, repair and grow. Every cell in your body was, at some point, derived from the food you consumed.

It's also true that 'food affects mood'. This is not just about Fido's instant pleasure hit when chowing down on a chunk of discarded steak fat. Food and its nutrients influence the brain at a far more fundamental level, shaping mood and behaviour.

Proteins consumed through food are further broken down into amino acids – they're like the little blocks that fit together to make up each protein. The body uses these amino acids for many things, including growing muscle, repairing tissue and making hormones and neurotransmitters.

Your mood and behaviours are regulated by brain chemistry. Neurotransmitters and hormones, the brain's chemical messengers, affect how brain cells work and communicate with each other. They dock into receptors in different parts of the brain, stimulating circuits to fire, which might then spark a particular feeling. For instance, serotonin is associated with feeling good and boosting mood, while dopamine is used by brain circuits that trigger feelings of pleasure and joy.

Take, for example, a detection dog trained to search for drugs. The dog is taught that every time it finds drugs, it wins a game with a ball that it really, really loves. These dogs are driven to work hard and search out the drugs so they can get the ball. When they do, they experience pleasure and joy through the activation in their brain's pleasure centre – the caudate nucleus. This part of the brain uses the neurotransmitter dopamine – it's a bit like the fuel that gets these brain circuits to work, and dopamine controls the circuits that fire to make the dog feel motivated. Now, whenever the dog starts to play the search game, it does so because it's anticipating the rewarding feeling of the ball at the end of it. Think of dopamine as fuel for the effort engine.

It makes sense then that nutrition can, in part, contribute to a dog's feelings and responses. A calm dog with a balanced mood is less likely to snap than one that struggles to control its impulses. Studies have backed this up by analysing the spinal fluid of aggressive dogs and found they had lower serotonin levels than other dogs.[2] This finding has been echoed in humans, too. A rather macabre study of murderers found lower serotonin levels in those who killed impulsively rather than pre-meditatively.[3] Serotonin keeps mood on an even keel and helps to suppress impulsive urges that can otherwise lead to emotional outbursts and lashing out.

Unexplained mood changes

Orwell, a rather energetic Spaniel-cross, had a dog dad who doted on him. Karl was a recently retired plumber, having spent the best part of half a century fixing leaky pipes all around Preston. He decided to give his ageing knees a break and hung up his tool belt, opting for a quieter life. But being a social person, it didn't take long before Karl missed his clients' chat and company. He and his wife had divorced some ten years earlier, and he had lived alone ever since. When his neighbour said they knew of a dog needing a home, Karl didn't hesitate to offer to take him on.

Orwell was only about two when Karl adopted him, and quickly became the main focus of his life. A failed search dog initially trained to find drugs in prison cells, Orwell was already pretty obedient and Karl loved taking him everywhere he went. He would often start the day with a walk up to the local café for a bacon sandwich. Of course, Orwell got the crusts, greedily gulping them down without even chewing.

After breakfast (which was more like brunch, given Karl didn't need to get up early any more), he and Orwell would take a leisurely walk to the pub, where they stayed for most of the day.

Karl liked a drink, but he liked the atmosphere in the pub more. He sat on the leather bench at the corner table with a good view of the bar and chatted to people he knew as they came in. He would slowly sip a pint of pale ale, reading the paper between the quips and banter he exchanged with the landlord as the latter poured drinks for the punters.

Orwell was a social pup and loved the pub as much as Karl. He would generally curl up next to Karl on the bench, placing his head in his dad's lap, nudging his hand for scritches behind his ear. He loved to roam around the bar, hunting for fuss and snacks. All the regulars knew him and readily indulged him. He was a gannet, though, and as soon as he heard a crisp packet open from the other side of the bar, he would shoot over, sit and beg, usually resulting in a pork scratching or two. He would wag his tail excitedly, as if he was dusting the floor, his front paws lightly tapping up and down like a drum roll, ready for the grand finale of catching whatever scraps he could.

When he was about five years old, something weird happened. Orwell started to get a little less social. Initially he was less interested in new people, but soon he started to growl whenever someone came over to say hello.[4]

Before long, he started barking and snapping at other dogs, too, despite having always been friendly and playful. Then, he started to become sensitive to loud noises– and not just loud bangs, like fireworks. He would bark at the kettle when Karl made a cuppa, especially when it started to boil. It even got to the point where Karl had to move the dog bed from the kitchen because the humming from the fridge would trigger Orwell.

Karl hadn't done anything differently. Orwell was still getting plenty of exercise and nothing had happened to make him change his behaviour. Karl couldn't understand it. He got a little nervous about Orwell being around other people and began tying him up to the table leg in the pub rather than letting him have the freedom he'd become accustomed to as the resident 'pub dog'.

Karl put it down to Orwell getting a bit grouchy in his old age (even though he wasn't that old). Until that is, one day, when the landlord came over to clear the glasses from the table and reached down to tickle Orwell under his chin. Orwell sat motionless, holding his gaze. The landlord thought that meant he was enjoying it and scratched him more, rubbing right the way down his neck to the tune of 'gooood booooy'. And then it happened. Suddenly, Orwell snapped at the landlord and took a chunk out of his thumb. Karl grabbed Orwell as the landlord leapt back in disbelief, checking his thumb to make sure it was still there.

Karl apologised, red-faced. He grabbed his coat and took Orwell home, letting the magnitude of what just happened sink in. He couldn't fathom what could have triggered Orwell's perpetual state of irritation. He was utterly terrified Orwell would be put down for biting, and that was just the impetus he needed to get on the front foot and deal with it. No more excuses. He wanted his Orwell back. The sweet, friendly Orwell – not the grizzly gremlin he'd somehow turned into.

Thinking it was a behavioural issue, he rang Danny, who listened intently to Karl's description of Orwell's changed behaviour. Because there hadn't seemed to be an obvious trigger, he suggested Karl take him to the vet first to ensure nothing was causing him pain before they started a training programme. Pain can be a common reason for a change in behaviour, so if Orwell had somehow got an ear infection or was suffering from a painful degenerative disease like arthritis, it might explain why he'd been getting progressively grouchier.

Karl took him to the vet and explained everything. The vet was sympathetic. She gently checked Orwell's ears and listened to his chest. She examined his teeth and, aside from a little bit of plaque, they seemed fine. She took some blood and urine samples, and all were normal. Karl called Danny back with the good news and they met for an assessment. But something still didn't seem quite right. Danny thought something deeper might be at play and suggested Karl take him back to the vet.

Several visits later, Orwell had been examined repeatedly, had his blood sampled, his urine analysed, and even his spinal fluid extracted and tested, and all of his results were completely unremarkable.

The vet was relentless, though, and insisted they keep looking for answers. She could see how much Orwell meant to Karl, and he couldn't risk another bite scenario. Eventually, Orwell was referred to a neurologist in case something was happening inside his brain, like a tumour, that might explain the changes in his behaviour. But, again, MRI scans showed everything to be normal.

Exasperated and with nothing to lose, the vet suggested trying a change in diet to see if that made any difference. She recalled being at a conference, where she'd had the opportunity to catch up with some old colleagues from her vet school days. They had mentioned hearing anecdotal evidence of dogs' behaviour improving in some cases following a diet change. It was a long shot because, at this point, there wasn't a great deal of research on diet and behaviour in dogs. She suggested putting Orwell on a gluten-free, hydrolysed protein diet. Hydrolysed protein is already broken down into constituent amino acids, making it easier to digest.

The results were encouraging. After a week, Orwell seemed a little less agitated. He still didn't like the kettle, but he didn't seem bothered by the fridge any more. Karl managed to hoover with Orwell just letting out a little grumble instead of launching a full-scale attack. Karl was encouraged, but wasn't taking anything for granted. He was still extremely careful with Orwell, avoiding situations where people might try to pet him.

Orwell started to be calmer when Karl took him out for walks, too. He was following Danny's training guidance around the way to deal with triggers and noticed Orwell seemed to be less reactive to other dogs, even tolerating a somewhat intrusive sniff from a curious Cockapoo outside the post office. He would settle on Karl's lap when they were at home watching TV. After three weeks, Orwell's aggression had reduced so much that he was pretty much back to how he used to be. Karl was astonished. (And even a little tempted to try the food himself!)

A couple of follow-up visits to the vet ensued, and subsequent blood tests found a clue. Orwell had higher than usual levels of a specific antibody that signalled a gluten sensitivity. The vet tested his poo and also found evidence of a condition where the intestines lose protein, meaning he wasn't getting the sustenance he needed.

It looked like Orwell had a gluten intolerance. His food had been leaving him feeling sore and miserable. It would be like one of us being allergic to dairy but having milk and cheese in every meal. We'd be left feeling bloated, crabby and with an achy stomach – it's enough to make anyone irritable. And in Orwell's case, this was playing a part. (As Karl discovered to his detriment a few months in when he forgot to order Orwell's special food and had to resort to standard dog food for a week, and Orwell started to get snappy again.)

Aside from impacting the intestinal tract, gluten sensitivity can also affect the gut–brain axis, which links the digestive system and the brain. The intestines are directly connected to the emotional and thinking parts of the brain, and they can communicate bidirectionally to affect each other's function.

Dogs aren't so dissimilar to people in this way. We know that for about 15 per cent of people with gluten intolerance – or celiac disease – the sensitivity can manifest as, for example, anxiety and depression. In these cases, a gluten-free diet has been shown to help, not just because it makes your stomach feel less upset but because it affects communication between the gut and the brain.

When the body is sensitive to gluten, it produces antibodies in response to gluten proteins. Antibodies usually target bacteria to stop them from spreading by attacking their cell wall or DNA. But these antibodies inadvertently target the nervous system and attack neurons – nerve and brain cells – and interfere with the systems the neurons use to communicate. Not only does gluten irritate the digestive tract, but it can also have a real and significant impact on the nervous system. It's one clear way for food to affect mood.

While gluten intolerance isn't that common in most dogs (although Irish Setters and Border Terriers are more prone to it genetically), it does show how important the interaction between the gut and the brain can be for how dogs feel and behave. Orwell's case wasn't common, and while diet can be a factor in behaviour, it's always important to consider it alongside a solid and tailored training programme.

Orwell's blood test results also showed that his intestines were losing protein. This was just as significant as the antibodies attacking his cells, although they acted on his system differently – and perhaps in a way that can more fundamentally affect all dogs.

All the proteins Orwell ate were broken down into their component amino acids. We heard earlier how the body uses these amino acids for many things, including making neurotransmitters. These chemical messengers in the brain help send messages between neurons. They're involved in switching circuits on and off and have an important role in controlling mood and behaviour. For example, serotonin helps control mood and sleep, while dopamine is important for feeling pleasure and motivation.

Feeding your dog's brain

As amino acids are the basic ingredients in cooking up neurotransmitters, it would make sense that a diet that alters the availability of these basic ingredients could subsequently affect behaviour. A group of scientists from the School of Veterinary Medicine at Tufts University in Massachusetts were particularly interested in the amino acid *tryptophan*, which produces serotonin in the brain – which you'll remember is the neurotransmitter linked to mood and behaviour.[5] They suspected that the amount of tryptophan in a dog's system limits its serotonin levels, and dogs with less serotonin are more likely to behave aggressively. They thought a diet with altered amounts of tryptophan could change aggressive behaviour in some (but not necessarily all) dogs.

The scientists chose to run this study using dogs with a history of aggression, as it's a trait known to be influenced by the amount of serotonin in a dog's brain. Each of the thirty-three dogs in the experiment were fed four different diets for one week each, with breaks in between.

The diets were either low-protein with and without tryptophan, or high-protein with and without tryptophan. Throughout the experiment, the scientists watched the dogs and recorded their behaviour daily to see if they were more or less aggressive depending on their diet. They also took blood samples to measure any change in serotonin and tryptophan levels.

As the scientists had predicted, the diets had a real impact on aggression. Adding tryptophan to both low- and high-protein diets reduced aggression, with the reduction particularly pronounced in low-protein diets. It seemed that adding tryptophan to the diet allowed more serotonin to be produced, which helped to stabilise mood and reduced aggressive reactions.

Low-protein diets were particularly effective because they changed the ratio of tryptophan to other amino acids in the body. In a high-protein diet, there was more competition between the various molecules trying to move from the blood to the brain. This happens at the blood–brain barrier, which acts like a protective shield around the brain. It's made up of tightly packed cells that line the blood vessels in the brain and allow essential nutrients to permeate and enter it while keeping germs and harmful substances out. It controls what can get into the brain from the bloodstream, acting as a 'smart filter'. In the case of the high-protein diet, the competition from other molecules at the barrier means less tryptophan gets into the brain, resulting in less serotonin. The low-protein diet seemed to provide a better balance of amino acids.

In Orwell's case, his later tests showed he was losing protein through his intestines. He wasn't able to absorb all the nutrients broken down from his food in the normal way. As well as the gluten-sensitive antibodies attacking his brain and nerve cells, it's possible that the ratio of amino acids in his body was also skewed. Orwell likely had a bad tummy, making him grouchy, and his low mood was compounded by having less tryptophan getting into the brain so less serotonin was produced. Serotonin is important for controlling impulses and regulating mood. If Orwell was feeling generally miserable already, and then something irritated him, he was more likely to lash out aggressively.

We're all so familiar with the importance of eating the right nutrients to keep a healthy body, but the impact of diet on a healthy mind is easily overlooked. Instead, we often see mood as something that's a purely psychological reaction to whatever we experience in the world. But the neurobiology of that process is of seismic importance. If the brain chemistry is imbalanced, the body lacks the fuel to feel pleasure or have a stable mood. Things we experience in the environment feel less good. Neurotransmitters are batteries that provide the energy source for these otherwise psychological traits.

This isn't to say a low-protein diet with a tryptophan supplement will work in every case of aggression. Many complexities affect how likely a dog is to be aggressive, both in terms of the behaviour learned, its genetics and, in this case, its brain chemistry. However, providing the right building blocks for healthy neurotransmitter levels might provide the stability a dog needs to allow an owner to work on its behaviour as part of a training programme.

Even when your dog has the optimum protein levels to give it enough tryptophan to make sufficient serotonin and, of course, the right balance of amino acids for crossing the blood–brain barrier, there are Omega-3s and Omega-6s to consider.

A group of researchers in Italy have found a link between levels of Omega-3 and Omega-6 and aggression in dogs.[6] Abnormal levels of lipids – or fats – have been linked with traits like hyperactivity, aggression and impulsiveness, all of which are also associated with serotonin levels.

They analysed blood samples from thirty-six German Shepherd dogs, half of which had a history of aggression, having attacked humans apparently 'without warning' (or rather, the warning signs were subtle and easily missed). The other half had no history of being aggressive.

The blood samples showed differences in the Omega-3 and Omega-6 fatty acid levels. Aggressive dogs had much lower Omega-3 levels and a much higher ratio of Omega-6 to Omega-3, which could affect the amount of serotonin in the brain. Rats fed a diet low in Omega-3s also had lower serotonin levels, and this dip can contribute to – but not necessarily cause – increased aggression.

The aggressive dogs also had less cholesterol, a type of waxy, fat-like substance that your body uses to build cell membranes and make certain hormones. While too much cholesterol is bad as it can lead to fatty deposits in the arteries, some is essential. In this case, low cholesterol could affect the production of serotonin, or it could be affecting the 're-uptake' process, where serotonin is reabsorbed back into brain cells after being released to send a message. This clears the neurotransmitter from the space between brain cells (the *synapse*), so the signal stops, and the chemicals can be recycled and used again. If these chemicals are not reabsorbed properly, it can affect how the brain cells fire, and there is less neurotransmitter available for the next time it's needed to turn the brain circuit on or off.

Lastly, aggressive dogs also had less bilirubin, which is produced when the body breaks down red blood cells. The connection between this and aggression is much less clear, but previous research indicates that bilirubin can have a protective effect on the brain. It could be this that somehow contributes to a dog being more likely to behave aggressively by stopping harmful substances like free radicals (unstable molecules that can build up in cells and cause damage) or rogue antibodies from attacking brain cells and interfering with the way they fire.

In Orwell's case, he was put on a strict diet that was especially suited to his gut health. As a consequence, it was likely better balanced, too, in terms of the nutrients and fats that he needed for his bodily health. In doing so, the right balance was also struck for his brain health. And while not all dogs would get such a dramatic improvement, diet could be a pinch point when it comes to mind as well as body.

There is a somewhat surprising amount of overlap between people and dogs regarding mood and food. The overlap extends to conditions such as Attention Deficit Hyperactivity Disorder – or ADHD – which dogs can also display. People with ADHD often have disruptions in their brain circuits that involve neurotransmitters like dopamine, noradrenaline and serotonin, which affect how they focus and control their impulses.

Some dogs display similar traits to humans with ADHD, such as being highly impulsive – think of the dog you know that can't wait for you to throw the ball without jumping up and mouthing it, despite extensive training. Not in a disobedient way, but more like a pathological way. They might also be the most energetic dogs you know – and we're not talking normal 'zoomies and drop', we're talking about constant hyperactivity.

A group of scientists in Helsinki collaborating from a number of research centres[7] were particularly interested in this kind of dog, given there could be similar disruptions to their brain circuits causing the behaviours. For example, a genetic variation that affects how dopamine is recycled back into nerve cells was found in Belgian Malinois[8] with high activity levels – which we know is a factor in humans with ADHD, where hyperactivity is also a commonly seen trait.

The team wanted to look at the role of the substances produced from breaking down lipids and amino acids, like tryptophan, which might affect ADHD-like behaviours in dogs, to see if they impacted them similarly to humans. They collected data on twenty-two German Shepherds, rating their levels of impulsivity and activity to ascertain how severe their ADHD-like behaviours were. To rule out anything erroneous, all dogs were fed the same diet for two weeks before blood samples were taken for analysis.

The dogs with more severe ADHD-like behaviours had lower levels of substances made by gut bacteria from breaking proteins down to release tryptophan, which we know is super-important for making neurotransmitters that regulate mood. These substances were *3-indolepropionic acid* and *indoleacetic acid*.

The acids indicate the amount of tryptophan the gut has broken down. They also have antioxidant properties, helping to protect cells from damage, and 3-indolepropionic acid can cross the blood–brain barrier and has a protective effect on brain and nerve cells.

So, lower levels of these acids in aggressive dogs might mean that damage to these cells results in them being more hyperactive and impulsive. The same traits could also cause changes in gut bacteria, which affect how well food is broken down. It's like having fewer of the right tools available to unscrew the nutrients from the bits of food being digested; instead, all the goodness gets pooed out. And the nervous system suffers as a result.

There was another point of interest with these dogs: those with higher ADHD scores also had higher levels of a substance called *kynurenic acid*. This is produced when bacteria in the gut break down tryptophan, meaning less is available in the system to cross the blood–brain barrier to make that all-important serotonin, which is super important in regulating impulsivity.

It's long been known that diet can help relieve ADHD symptoms in humans. A 'ketogenic' diet that is high in fat, low in protein and low in carbohydrates has been particularly successful.

A group of researchers based in the UK, led by Rowena Packer of the Royal Veterinary College, wanted to explore whether the same kind of diet could help dogs with ADHD traits.[9] Over six months, they collected data on twenty-one dogs. They were all fed a ketogenic diet and a plain diet for a period of three months each, and their behaviour was compared.

Similar to people, the keto diet seemed to help to alleviate some of the symptoms. After three months of keto, the dogs were less likely to chase and were much less afraid of strangers. They seemed more readily trainable, probably because they could better focus on their owners without distraction.

The keto diet changed the balance of what was going into the dog's system in a way that made a difference to their brain chemistry. It might be that the keto diet affected the way that tryptophan is broken down to make it more readily available to make serotonin. We also know that the ratio of different kinds of fats can affect serotonin production, so it could be that the high-fat and low-protein diet helped here, too, contributing to better-balanced brain chemistry and behavioural improvements.

Sadly there isn't a silver bullet of a diet that will make any dog behave impeccably. Behaviour is influenced by many factors – many of them will be the dog's experiences to date and how different behaviours have succeeded, or not. For example, if a dog feels threatened and snaps at someone to try and put a bit of distance between them, and said person backs away, the dog will learn that snapping works to get rid of people. Genetics also matter – some dogs might have a huge amount of motivation. If they don't get enough stimulation, they can become aggressive, like a Collie chasing shadows around the house because it's not got anything appropriate to chase as an outlet for this genetic need.

If there were a magic diet that would instantly fix these problems, we would undoubtedly have all our dogs on it by now. The causes of behaviours are so complex that it would be disingenuous to suggest that the right diet will powerfully change your dog's thinking. But, in theory, it should be possible to influence behaviour with diet. At the very least, it would give your dog the right fuel for the brain circuits it needs to function well. These fuel levels make certain behaviours more or less likely to happen. So, a well-fuelled brain gives you the best chance of changing those behaviours.

Many of us can relate to days when our brains aren't well fuelled – the brain fog, the tiredness, the difficulty focusing. When we feel like this, we have the gift of language to communicate our feelings. We can say, 'Sorry – I don't mean to be snappy; I'm really not feeling that great.' Dogs don't have that luxury and are left with the only option of reacting – usually aggressively – to let us know that they're unhappy.

A good, balanced diet, rich in the building blocks needed for good brain health, reduces the likelihood of impulsive and aggressive behaviour and reduces stress. One study by scientists working across Italy, and in Florida, USA, found that a diet enhanced with a range of supplements, like fish proteins, various plant extracts and additional amino acids, reduces the levels of stress markers in the blood after just forty-five days.[10] This is probably because having the right fuel in the brain (there were also increased serotonin, dopamine and noradrenaline levels) meant that the dogs felt more relaxed and were more able to cope with the world.

It's not that any particular food stops the world from being stressful; it's just that the balance of food means the dog is better protected. Wearing a coat in the rain won't stop it from being wet outside, but you'll be less likely to feel soggy than if you went out without that protective layer. In this case, the right fuel for the brain gives that bit of protection and offers the best chance of dealing with the world.

There are many different kinds of food you can give to your dog. Choosing the right diet is personal to you, your circumstances and – of course – your wallet. There is no hard-and-fast rule, or any particular diet that is best. If you're struggling with aggressive or impulsive

WHAT YOUR DOG IS THINKING

behaviours that you can't seem to resolve through training alone, speak to your vet about trying a low-protein diet with appropriate tryptophan, Omega-3 and Omega-6 supplements.

Orwell was a much happier dog after changing his food, although Danny and Karl still had some work to do addressing his issues as Orwell had practised them for so long they became habits. Even though he felt better, he needed a bit of help to change his responses.

So far, we've concentrated on fixing problem behaviours. Next, let's have some fun.

Try this: Use food to teach your dog to find things
We've focused this chapter on the value of diet in feeding your dog's brain. But you can also use it to feed your dog's mind as a reward for a task or a game you can teach it that it enjoys and finds stimulating. This one is also intensely practical, as you will teach your dog to search out a lost item with its nose.

With this method, you can train your dog to find anything you like, but you must teach each item individually. We recommend anything you have a habit of misplacing, like your phone, your wallet or your keys. The great thing about this method is that you can teach it from the comfort of your own home.

You first need a container in which to place your chosen object – in this case, your keys. It should be big enough to contain your object but sturdy enough that your dog can't reach it. The container also needs to have holes in its surface so that the dog can get the object's scent. You don't need anything special for this. Danny likes to get a couple of the shakers used to sprinkle chocolate on cappuccinos. But a glass jam jar, or even a plastic box, with holes pierced in the lid, will also do.

Ensure that whatever you use is cleaned thoroughly to prevent other scents from contaminating the item you want to train your dog to find. Remember, dogs use smell as their primary sense, and their noses are super-sensitive.

Before we do this, we will assume that your dog already knows the word that tells it that it's done something right and will be rewarded. If not, you can do this by repeatedly saying 'yes' and then giving your dog a reward, like a bit of food. This is called 'charging up a mark' because you're charging the 'mark' (in this case the word 'yes') to be linked in your dog's mind with a reward (see Chapter 1).

Now, take your container and place a little piece of food inside it. It can be anything your dog really likes – a bit of smelly cheese, a piece of cooked meat or its favourite treat.* Place the container in the middle of the room so your dog can see it easily and get plenty of whiffs through the holes. Without you saying anything to encourage your dog, it will pique your dog's curiosity, and all you need to do is wait for your dog to sniff it, then say 'yes' and reward your dog for showing interest. When you reward it in this exercise, throw the treat on the floor near the container because it helps your dog to link the container it showed interest in with the reward. They will have a stronger association in this way.

Repeat this until your dog clearly understands that going to the container and sniffing it will result in a reward. You'll know when your dog is at this point because it will go straight to the container and show interest in it. Some dogs might look back, expecting the reward. If your dog does this, wait until it looks at the container again before rewarding it so that it is clear that

---

* If your dog is more toy-motivated you could also cut off a piece of its toy and put that in the jar instead of the food, and reward it with the toy. Trainers of search dogs tend to use toys instead of food to avoid the dogs mistaking discarded food on the floor of search sites as a reward.

the container is what gets it the treat (and not just running to the same spot).

Now that your dog links the container and its smell with getting a reward, it's time to introduce the command, or 'cue' you want to use to get it to search for something. It's important not to do this step too early; the dog must first make that all-important link with the container and a reward for sniffing it.

Pop your dog on a loose lead, long enough for it to be able to reach the container but still giving you the ability to control it. Now say your chosen 'cue' word. Let's go with 'find it'. Ensure the dog has enough slack to reach the container, and when it sniffs it, mark it with 'yes' and reward it. Repeat this until your dog is proficient, and as soon as it hears the cue, it heads straight to the container. You might need to do this over several sessions to be confident your dog has got the hang of it. As always, patience and practice are the key ingredients whenever you teach your dog something new.

Next, it's time to step the challenge up a level. We're now going to add a second empty container. Make sure that it's completely clean and has no trace of the scent of the food you're using in the first container. Place the second container two feet or so away from the first one (with the food inside). Have your dog about six or seven paces away, if you have that much space, and tell your dog 'find it'. Then give some slack in the lead.*

Then, wait for your dog to go to the container with the scent, mark 'yes,' and reward it. It might take a while initially, and your dog might go to the wrong one or look a bit confused

---

* It's important to say 'find it' before you give slack in the lead so that your dog doesn't confuse the action of dropping the lead with being the cue to start searching.

because it doesn't yet fully understand that finding the food smell – rather than the container – equals the reward. Don't repeat the command; just be patient and give your dog time to work it out for itself.

Keep going with this for a while, and every so often, put your dog away so that it can't see what you're doing. Move the containers to a different position to make the game more challenging.

We build up gradually to introduce a third container, then a fourth and a fifth. Starting with three containers, line these up against a wall with a good gap between them, still with food in only one. Say 'find it' and walk your dog on a lead along the wall, allowing it to sniff as it passes each container until it finds the one with the food in it. When it does, mark with 'yes' and throw its food near that container. Every so often, move the containers around so your dog is 'finding' the scent in a new location. This makes sure the dog is learning that finding the scent produces the reward, not just moving to a particular spot.

Now that your dog knows that it must find the scent to win the game, it's time to introduce an action we want it to take when it finds it. This is called an 'indication'. Next, when you walk your dog along the wall and it finds the right container, tell it to sit. As soon as it does, mark with 'yes' and throw the food. Repeat this until your dog automatically finds and then sits next to the scent. This will likely take a few sessions to become really well ingrained.

The next advancement to the game will involve changing the placement of the containers. This time, place them in the shape of a letter 'N'. Make sure there is enough space for your dog to move between the containers. Now choose a side to start at and say 'find it'. Slacken off the lead and walk the dog around the shape in a methodical way, and search the containers for the

scent. You can do this on or off the lead – some dogs might be over-excited and knock the containers over while they search.*
Keep switching up the position of the containers so the dog actively sniffs out the right one, rather than just remembering the location of the winning container.

Once your dog can confidently search out the scent, sit and wait for a reward, it's time for the exciting bit – introducing the scent of whatever you want your dog to find. We're going with keys. Keys are metal, so your dog will learn to sniff out anything metallic if you use your keys. If you want to give your dog a head start in finding your particular bunch of keys, you could add a specific scent, such as by using a leather keyring. Then, your dog will sniff out the combination of metal and leather.

Whatever you choose to use, pop it in the container with a smaller piece of food and keep repeating the exercise with multiple containers lined up against a wall, as before. Once your dog is proficient in that, you can wash out the container so there's no scent of the food – or use a fresh one – and just put the keys in there and continue to repeat the exercise. This weans your dog away from smelling out the food to get a reward, and now it learns that finding the keys produces the reward.

Keep switching your sessions between the wall and the 'N' exercises and using different rooms and locations to generalise the concept. Just keep mixing up the position of the container with the keys in it and be patient. It might take a few weeks for your dog to get really proficient. There's no set time limit on how long this should take. It will differ for each dog. You want

---

* If your dog is knocking over the containers, you can stand them up using makeshift stands. A piece of guttering with holes cut out works particularly well.

to get to the stage where you can put your containers in any room, and your dog will search for them, find them and sit, ready to be rewarded.

Now that your dog has the concept of searching for a specific scent, we're going to teach it how to search a room systematically. This might be the difference between finding keys that have slid behind a table and missing them completely. You're going to need at least eight containers – one in each corner of the room, and one by each piece of furniture or in the centre of each wall. The idea is that they frame the entire room and encourage your dog to search all around it.

Pop your dog on a lead so you can guide it around the room, starting at the door. Tell your dog to 'find it', and either go left or right, searching the entire perimeter of the room, rewarding it when it sits at the right container. If your dog guesses and sits at the wrong container, wait it out until it finds the right one.

Continue practising this by changing the container's location and searching different rooms. Gradually, you can start to make this more challenging by putting containers a bit higher up, on top of a table, or wedging them in a drawer. Get creative!

You might have to do this for a few weeks until your dog is confident. Then, it's time to phase out the containers. Remove all the containers and just put the keys somewhere on their own. Initially, don't make it too hard. Make sure it's a familiar place – you want your dog to succeed and learn that the game has moved on, and that containers are no longer in play. Keep repeating, gradually increasing the challenge by hiding the keys in different places, then in different rooms and different locations.

Just because dogs have extremely powerful olfactory systems and are really sensitive to smell doesn't mean they'll automatically be brilliant at finding things. Even some dogs that are bred specifically for scent work have to work at it. Searching through scent is a skill your dog needs to acquire, just like a child learning to play football. Start small and build up those skills. Some are naturally talented search dogs, and some will need more practice. They should get there if you are using a reward they're motivated to find.

There are lots of ways to teach scent work to a dog. This exercise provides a step-by-step methodical and clear guide that should work for any dog. Be patient and consistent, and rest safe, knowing you'll never lose your keys again.

Summary
- Food can influence your dog's mood by providing more or less of the building blocks it needs to make neurotransmitters. These provide the fuel for the communication system in your dog's brain, allowing brain cells to talk to each other and information to flow through different parts of the brain.
- The neurotransmitter serotonin is important for regulating mood. Dogs without enough serotonin can be aggressive and impulsive. Tryptophan is a key amino acid involved in making serotonin. Diets rich in tryptophan, particularly when combined with lower levels of protein, result in more tryptophan getting into the brain to produce higher levels of serotonin, which could reduce aggression in some cases.
- The amount of Omega-3s and the ratio of Omega-3s to Omega-6s also influence the amount of serotonin produced.
- Many complex reasons cause dogs to express aggression. Aggressive behaviours should be dealt with through a solid and tailored behavioural programme. However, a healthy

diet, balanced to provide optimum brain health, can help to balance brain chemistry and may, in some cases, reduce the likelihood of aggression.

- Food can be used to teach your dog to find an object of your choosing.
- Start small with a piece of food in a container with holes in it, enabling scent to escape. Allow your dog to make an association with that smell and being rewarded. Then introduce the cue, 'find it'. Next add in an empty container and reward your dog when it goes to the one with food inside.
- Gradually increase the number of additional empty containers, then teach your dog to sit to indicate it has found the food. Continue to repeat with containers lined up against a wall and in the shape of an 'N', changing the location of the container with the food.
- Introduce the object (like keys) to be searched for by adding it to the container with the food and repeat the exercises until the dog is proficient. Then gradually remove the food and leave only the item in the container. Then, move the containers to the perimeter of a room to teach your dog to search any given room systematically. Once proficient, remove the container and allow your dog to search for the keys. Repeat in various rooms and locations to ensure your dog generalises the behaviour.

Chapter 8

What your dog is thinking when it looks guilty

Ralph had been on his own for ages. Simon, his owner, worked long hours in an office, and Ralph was often left to entertain himself for most of the day. He didn't mind too much. He was a little bit lazy and loved to sleep, but once he'd had enough napping, he tended to get bored. Especially late in the afternoon, when he started to need a pee, prompting him to get restless.

In Ralph's case, restlessness meant mischievousness. He usually found something inappropriate to tear up, earning him the nickname 'Wreck-it Ralph'. As a large and unusual-looking albino bull-breed with a thick-set head and stocky body, the name suited him.

Ralph stirred from his spot on the sofa, feeling a tingle in his bladder that he knew from experience he couldn't relieve for at least a few more hours. He sat upright and stretched his neck, pointing his pink, wrinkly nose towards the ceiling. As he relaxed his stretch, he yawned, licking his lips a few times as if to clear away the sticky spit of his slumber.

Slowly, he clambered down from the sofa, knocking all but one of the cushions he was nestled amongst onto the floor. Ralph was oblivious to his size. His profound lack of spatial awareness meant he would often leave a trail of destruction behind him.

He paused, and his nose twitched. He could smell something. He raised his head a little higher as he sniffed the air, hoping to catch a few more molecules of whatever that delectable scent was. Dogs have incredibly sensitive olfactory systems, with over 100 million smell receptors in their noses compared to just six million in humans. They can detect a single drop of blood in water in an area the size of two Olympic swimming pools.

Ralph sniffed again. It smelt like Simon's dinner from last night: chicken. He was sure it was chicken – possibly with a dash of fermented cod. That was probably from lunch two days earlier. Simon had been a bit slow in taking out the rubbish, which meant one thing to Ralph: pungent-smelling treasure.

He plodded to the kitchen, his white, whippy tail gently swaying back and forth as he sashayed in. The smell was getting stronger, enticing him towards the bin in the corner of the room. He trotted over, glancing momentarily (and longingly) at the patio door as his bladder tingled again. Undeterred, he continued to the holy grail of his mission: the kitchen bin.

Ralph approached the bin, sniffing ever more intensely. The scent of even more tasty morsels filled his nasal cavity and tickled his excitement. He sniffed it up and down, searching for where the odour was most potent, pointing to a way in. The silver metal was cold against his nose, snotty streaks smeared up and down the barrel.

Ralph stood on his hind legs to get a better sniff at the top of the bin, and pawed at the black plastic lid. His claws caught between the lid and the barrel, and with a few strokes, he prised it off. It tumbled to the floor, rolling away and coming to rest by a chair leg at the kitchen table.

With his nose in the bin, Ralph was hit with a wall of smells – so much more than just chicken and cod. There were stale bread rinds, a couple of rotten strawberries, some bean juice, and what can only be described as the dregs of a not-so-smoothie. Ralph couldn't wait to get whatever was hitting his nose into his mouth. With his paws on the lip of the bin, he stretched himself as far as he could to get his fat, chunky head deep inside.

Scraping a back paw against the bin for purchase, he tried hard to reach the source of the smells. He nipped the corner of a bread bag and tugged it a bit. It loosened the waste a little, but really, it just re-jumbled the jumble. It didn't bring up any food treats. He tried again, gripping any odd bit of refuse in his mouth, hoping it would produce some bounty. His back paw kicked and scraped the bin, but instead of giving leverage, the bin gave way and tumbled on top of him. Ralph fell backwards, twisting, landing heavily, half on his back and half on his side.

Ralph didn't care that it hurt. To him, the joy of the bin hunt superseded the pain of falling awkwardly. An equation played out in Ralph's brain: value, minus effort and discomfort. The value of tearing up the bin was pretty high, say a ten, minus the effort – which Ralph didn't mind, so about a two – and the discomfort of falling, which was another two, equalling what he would do next. The plus side was ten, but the minuses were only four. The discomfort wasn't great enough to outweigh the behaviour's value, so he prevailed.

He leapt back up, the treasure chest now open and showering its goods all over the floor. Elated, Ralph ploughed through the rubbish, tearing up empty packets and licking any last remnants of flavour. He found the rotten strawberries and gulped them without chewing. They had a bit of a kick, presumably from the fermented fruit sugars – not that it stopped Ralph.

Ecstatic, Ralph continued to go through the bin, consuming scraps and tearing up everything else like a wolf dissecting flesh from the bones of a kill. He was in his element. Scraps of rubbish covered the floor, swept further afield by his excited paws and swooshing tail. Not content with simply going through the rubbish, Ralph pushed his head back into the bin, tentatively crawling into it like a cave. He could still smell goodness. He started to tug at the bin bag itself. It had been marinaded in bin juice, and to Ralph, that was a delicacy.

After a good forty minutes of munching, Ralph was satisfied he had pretty much everything he wanted from the bin. The mission had somewhat overtaken the sensation that he had to pee, and he'd almost forgotten about it until he stopped smashing through the trash.

Then, the tingling in his bladder returned, and he looked through the patio doors again at the garden. He wished he could get out there. After pacing around the table three times, his attention was caught by a Babybel rind, and he went back to chewing on his rubbish pile. He lay down on top of the mess, holding the rind between his front paws, and gently mauled at it. Bits of red wax stuck to his teeth like lipstick on your gran's incisors. Nevertheless, he was very happy to spend the rest of the afternoon chewing through his pile of rubbish.

A few hours later, Simon returned home from a long day at work. Ralph's head shot up as he heard the key in the front door, and his tail wagged furiously, sending remnants of packaging flying across the floor. He barked to say, 'Dad! You're home!' and leapt up excitedly, ready to greet him.

But as Simon walked in, Ralph quickly realised he was unhappy. In fact, unhappy was an understatement. Simon was furious. His face creased with indignation, and he raised his fists above his head, gesticulating wildly.

'For fuck's sake, Ralph! Not again! Why the hell do you do this, every fucking time!' he ranted, incandescent with rage and almost incoherent, a torrent of profanity-laden words exploding out of his mouth.

Ralph didn't appear to like it when Simon shouted like this. He wanted it to stop. He gingerly approached Simon with his head bowed low. He cautiously took a few steps towards him, licking his lips a few times as he did so, which infuriated Simon even more. He was affronted because he thought it was a sign that whatever Ralph ate was tasty. And he shouldn't have eaten it! Ralph looked away and back to Simon, then away again, trying to show him that he was not being adversarial. His tail was carried low between his hind legs, and his ears were back, almost flat.

To Simon, Ralph looked guilty as sin. He knew Ralph was well aware of the rules. He'd told him off countless times before for tearing up the bin. He must know. Simon was seething.

But was Ralph displaying guilt? Despite being reprimanded for the same crime previously, had Ralph learned that the bin shouldn't be ripped open and had therefore deliberately ignored Simon's authority? Instead, choosing the momentary pleasure of the bin juice over Simon's legitimate and inevitable wrath?

The complexity of guilt

Regrettably, most of us know what it is to feel guilty about something, whether a minor transgression, like forgetting to reply to a friend's text message for so long it now feels rude even to open it, or something more significant, like arguing with a dying relative and leaving it too late to make up. Whatever the trigger, we all know that gut-wrenching ache of regret.

Guilt is a super-complex emotion, which is important when considering the evidence for whether dogs can experience it. Every emotion we feel originates in a series of actions and subsequent chemical reactions inside our brains. And a lot happens inside the brain when something flicks the guilt switch.

Guilt is grounded in an ability to hold onto concepts about normal social behaviours. When you feel guilt, you feel something about a moral sentiment – an emotion. Guilt doesn't feel good. But that negative feeling is also overlaid with a much more abstract concept of social values – you've transgressed a moral or a social rule. You must understand right from wrong and where your behaviours sit within those categories. This requires you to reason, which takes a lot of brain power and advanced brain structures that only humans seem to have.

But guilt also depends on the sequence of events. If you lose your temper with someone, you might feel bad. But if that person kicked your dog before you lost your temper with them, I doubt you'd feel so rubbish. In this case, many would argue that losing your temper was justified. The judgement of that transgression is dependent on the order of events. When you experience guilt, there is activity in the thinking engine of your brain (the ventral prefrontal cortex) that you use when you consider the order in which things happen.

There is much discussion about whether dogs can feel guilt. But as you can see, a lot happens when humans experience it, particularly wondering whether an action was justified, even if it breaks social norms. Something that triggers guilt in one context may not automatically trigger guilt in another.

Brain imaging experiments have shown that when you feel guilt, you use parts of your brain, such as the *mesolimbic* and *forebrain* areas, to feel emotion and represent social concepts.[1] Humans have a relatively large forebrain – taking up about a third of the brain – which allows us to do this. That gives us our processing power and the ability to think like we do.

However, dogs have a much smaller frontal lobe, taking up a tiny 10 per cent. They're less able to reason and think rationally. So, holding the concepts needed to feel guilt will not be easy for a dog. They might feel a rudimentary type of regret or sadness, but they likely don't have the brain machinery necessary to feel guilty about doing something wrong.

When Ralph was zealously turfing through the rubbish, he probably wasn't thinking, 'I really shouldn't', or 'Simon will go mad'. He was unlikely to think he was doing anything that would upset Simon, which he should therefore not do; and by doing it anyway, he was being bad and should, thus, feel guilty.

That doesn't detract from the fact that Ralph *looked* guilty. When people feel guilty, they bow their heads and make themselves small.

Their facial expressions change, and they avoid eye contact. Ralph looked like a person would look when they felt guilty.

The truth behind those guilty looks

It's no surprise that most people think that their dog's reactions when caught doing something wrong are signs of guilt. More than nine out of ten people believe their dogs show guilt and, therefore, have this clear moral understanding of right from wrong. But if dogs don't have the brain machinery to feel guilt, what is that guilty look about?

A team of scientists in Budapest in Hungary, and Scotland, have been keen to understand this question and have set up an experiment to see whether dogs express remorse when changing their demeanour, or if something else might trigger the behaviours.

They used sixty-four dogs and put them in a room, one by one. Each dog had the chance to eat some food left on a table in the room, despite being trained not to 'steal' it.[2] As expected, some dogs would steal it, and others wouldn't. But the scientists didn't find any difference in behaviours – the dogs didn't look guilty or apprehensive right before swiping the treat. If they felt guilty about it, you'd imagine their demeanour might betray them right at the point of theft. If they understood that they were doing something naughty, you would expect them to look at least a little sheepish.

Having said that, we might feel guilty on the *inside* when we take the last bit of cake out of the fridge – despite it belonging to our child, who we knew was saving it and looking forward to it. But we're unlikely at that point to *look* guilty if no one is around. We might have made sure there was no one around, thus avoiding any eye contact, and we wouldn't change our posture to reflect our mood. What if dogs feel guilty but don't display it when they do a misdeed because there is no one there to see it?

Alexandra Horowitz, a psychologist from Barnard College in New York City, set up an experiment to disentangle whether dogs' 'guilty looks' are indeed due to a guilty feeling or whether the dogs might be changing their behaviours in response to the environment.[3]

She put the dogs through several trials. As in the last experiment, the dogs were placed in a room with their owners, who told them not to eat a particularly tasty-looking treat. The owners were told it was a test of obedience, so they didn't inadvertently focus on guilt in a way that might have influenced their dogs. They then left the room, and the dogs had the chance to eat the treat – or not.

Alexandra threw in a twist: sometimes, she would take the treat herself, so when the owners came back into the room, they had no idea it wasn't the dog that took it. They were told either to scold the dogs if there was no treat or to greet them nicely if there was, and Alexandra studied their dogs' reactions to see whether anything changed their 'guilty' looks.

Once again, the dogs didn't show any more 'guilty' looks after stealing the treat than when they obeyed. In fact, the determining factor that triggered the dogs' guilty faces was being scolded by their owners. It wasn't a reliable sign that they'd done something wrong – because, as we know, Alexandra was sometimes stealing the treats – and when they were scolded but hadn't done anything to be guilty about, they still looked guilty.

When scolded, dogs display guilty behaviours similar to submissive behaviours, such as avoiding eye contact or lowering their body. These are probably behaviours they've learned in the past. They've likely experienced their owners being cross and found that being submissive stops the anger response. The owner calms down because they can see the dog looks 'guilty' and by extension 'remorseful'. So, the dog learns that doing this stops the scolding. Dogs display the exact same submissive demeanour when another dog reprimands them. They want to appease them to say sorry, and they don't want the conflict to continue. In Ralph's case, he had no idea what he did was wrong. He just wanted Simon to stop shouting at him, which triggered his guilty look.

It's so easy to misinterpret these behaviours as guilt because they look like we would if we were guilty of a misdemeanour. But they're not tied in the dog's mind to anything they've done. It's more about your dog avoiding you being angry with it than any understanding of wrongdoing. However, these behaviours affect how the dog and person interact, and people's expectations about their dog's understanding of right and wrong.

Some people might see their dogs responding before they're scolded. Although the study did not find that, there could still be some truth in it. If a dog has had previous scoldings in the presence of the bin bag, dished out by the human, it can link the bin bag and the human with that scolding, which triggers the guilty looks. It's as simple as 'ripped bin bag plus human equals anger'. Therefore, the dog responds submissively to counter that anger. It's not the same as the dog understanding that the action of ripping open the bin bag was the transgression that would cause the upset. Dogs don't have the brain structure to compute the latter, but they are super-sensitive to context. They know that this context leads to tension, and they don't want us to be angry; they want us to be friends.

It's also entirely plausible that dogs look a bit sheepish because they're upset that they're being stopped from doing something they enjoy. To Ralph, ripping open the bin bag was fun. He revelled in the stinky pile of rubbish. He had a similar submissive reaction when Simon told him to get off the chair that he perched on to look out of the window. He would look sheepishly at Simon as the latter pointed at the floor, not because he felt bad that he was somewhere he wasn't supposed to be, but because he liked looking out the window. It held value to him. So, in his eyes, Simon was taking something valuable away. Ralph wasn't looking guilty. He was just a bit gutted.

There were similar incidents with the armchair. The first week that Simon had Ralph at home, as an adolescent dog fresh from the shelter, he left him alone while he went to work and came home to sofa guts strewn across the room. Ralph had destroyed the blue velvet armchair, pulling off all the tufted buttons, tearing the fabric and exposing sofa foam and fluff. He then proceeded to gnarl his way through that. It was carnage.

When Simon saw his beloved chair in pieces, he inevitably lost his temper. Ralph had the same guilty-looking reaction we talked about earlier, which convinced Simon that he knew he had done wrong. Unbeknown to Simon, Ralph had been set up to fail.

At the rescue shelter, each dog kennel had a furniture item in it. Ralph's kennel had an armchair. Others had a small sofa or cushions placed around their dog beds. The staff at the shelter wanted to prepare dogs for going into a home environment. They believed that providing some creature comforts in their kennels would get the dogs used to the environment in a home, and so they would relax into their new surroundings more quickly.

The kennel staff were well-meaning, but adding soft furnishings to the kennels gave dogs an outlet for their boredom and stress. They would rip up the bits of furniture, and they were permitted to do so.

Most dogs have an innate desire to shred things. It's part of the 'predatory cycle' of behaviours they would use to chase, catch, kill and dissect their prey to eat it. That's why sometimes dogs will eat weird objects that aren't food. It's not unlike our hunter-gatherer tendencies, which in modern times are satisfied by shopping and collecting things instead of hunting and foraging. We can't help enjoying it. It feels instinctively good.

Ralph started destroying the furniture in the kennels because he was bored and found it innately satisfying. No one told him off because it was just an old chair. When he moved in with Simon, he saw the armchair and thought it was great! He had something to enjoy ripping up. He had no concept he was doing anything wrong. He had been allowed to practise a behaviour without understanding it was a serious misdemeanour.

The idea of creating an environment that helps dogs transition to their new lives is a sound one. The issue was more that it was being done through the eyes of a human rather than through the eyes of a dog. A person would think 'a lovely comfy sofa', whereas a dog would think 'something to tear up'. Humans have such strong empathetic tendencies that we quickly try to look at the world through the eyes of another. The problem happens when we look at something from a dog's point of view through an unhelpfully human lens. We see the world through our own perspective. So, we see the dog's world through our own learned experiences.

This human trait might bias us to see the worst in our dogs and attribute blame. As people, we tend to recognise human-esque characteristics in everything, like seeing faces in clouds or vegetables shaped like slightly rude body parts. We have a tendency to attribute similar human qualities to animals – we anthropomorphise them.

It could be as simple as thinking a dog looks like it's smiling when it's panting, or hugging your dog because you assume it will enjoy it as a sign of affection. It's even easier to think that dogs can feel the same way we do. It's unsurprising that so many people believe their dogs feel guilty when they look guilty and are worthy of a reprimand.

There is evidence that this is driven purely by how we see ourselves. A study conducted by Christina Brown and Julia McLean at Arcadia University, Pennsylvania, USA, examined how people project their personality traits onto their dogs.[4] People were asked to interpret ambiguous dog behaviours that could suggest guilt, like knocking over a plate and avoiding eye contact; loneliness, like watching the door when no one is home; or anxiety, like pacing back and forth. The researchers also took human personality assessments, and it turns out that people prone to feeling guilty were more likely to see guilt and anxiety in their dogs.

When dogs lower their heads and sheepishly avoid eye contact, guilt-prone people tend to think that is a sign of guilt. They are more likely to project their own emotions onto their dogs because that is how they would tend to respond if they felt guilty. Because they often felt guilty, they were sensitive to it as it was so familiar.

We all tend to use our own emotional experiences to fill in the gaps when we encounter a situation. Because dogs can't tell us how they're feeling, every situation has an echo of ambiguity. They can't come over and say, 'Hey, I'm really sorry. I know I shouldn't have ripped the bin bag open, but I just couldn't help it,' or more likely, 'Oh no, you look cross? Why are you cross? Please don't shout at me, I don't like it when you're angry.' We see their behaviour, which is a sign of the latter, and use our own experiences to make us assume the former.

In some ways, anthropomorphising our dogs is a sign of empathy – we want to think about how they're feeling so we can better help them. But our only frame of reference is our own, and that can be very different from theirs. It's important to pause, take a deep breath, and think about things from our dogs' point of view and, indeed, through their eyes.

Another human comparison we tend to make with our dogs is more aligned to human guilt and whether or not we're being sufficiently good 'dog parents'. This was something that bothered Simon a lot. He worked long hours for a particularly inflexible corporation that wouldn't permit him to work from home. He felt an immense pressure to be 'present'. He was judged not only on sales targets but also on how available he was to his boss. And that meant staying in her eyeline all the time.

He seldom left work before six in the evening on a weekday. To cope with the high-pressure, high-stakes office environment, Simon had a busy social calendar. He would often pop home, let Ralph out, change and then go back out to meet friends for a few drinks.

He knew he wasn't as present for Ralph as he should be. Sometimes, days would go by, and Simon would realise he hadn't taken him for a walk since the weekend. He felt terrible. His tendency to feel guilty may have made him more likely to see Ralph's behaviours as guilty.

To be fair to Simon, we all experience competing demands. Sometimes, we feel bad that we have to work late and our dogs are stuck at home all day, or we don't feel great and skip their walk. The guilt we feel when our responsibilities interfere with the time we spend with our dogs mirrors the kind of guilt parents feel about their children when they get tied up in the same way.

A study in the USA entitled 'Disenfranchised Guilt—Pet Owners' Burden' led by Lori Kogan involved nearly six hundred dog owners, and measured various aspects of their guilt.[5] It considered their view of an ideal dog owner and compared it to how they viewed themselves. It also looked at how attached they felt to their dogs and how other responsibilities distracted them from giving their dogs what they needed. The study used a scale to assess the level of guilt the owners felt and its cognitive and emotional features, similar to those of parents and their children.

Many of us see our dogs as fully-fledged members of our families. We look after all their needs, whether physical, like feeding them; psychological, like teaching them things; or financial, by paying for everything they need. We bring them up and care for them. They are dependants, like children.

It is no surprise, but the study found that dog owners experience similar guilt to that reported by parents, particularly concerning how work interferes with family – or dog – time. Owners felt torn between work commitments and the time they wished to spend with their pets in an ideal world. The guilt can be intense, really affecting how people feel – it can be upsetting to think you're letting your dog down.

People would try to compensate to alleviate their guilt, such as saying no to social events because they felt bad for leaving their dogs at home. Perhaps there's merit in this, and it's about time we normalised bringing our dogs as our plus one. It reflects the significant emotional investment we put into our dogs and the lengths to which people will go to relieve their guilt.

We all experience tension between the people we are and the people we would ideally like to be. In an ideal world, we want to be with our dogs twenty-four hours a day, seven days a week, train them perfectly, take them on three walks a day and have a home free from rogue dog hair. The reality might be closer to one walk a day, reasonable lead walking skills, and the odd human lapse when we're cross that our mutt chewed up our favourite trainers. We feel guilt when we don't live up to our own expectations – regardless of how unrealistic they might be.

It may be time for more workplaces to acknowledge the very real impact of animal–human relationships. We might not reach our 'ideal dog parent' status, but we could at least find practical ways to relieve the tension. The guilt people experience about their dogs is real, as is the grief when we lose a dog. With a little more patience and practical consideration, we can all be a bit more human.

Try this: Stop your dog from indulging in destructive behaviour
When your dog goes through the bin, it's not just a mess issue; it's a potential safety issue. We throw things away that can be harmful to dogs, including food scraps that are toxic to them, like onions, raisins, grapes and even chocolate. Ralph was lucky that the chicken he found in the bin was breast meat; had it been bones, they could have splintered in his gut and made him seriously ill. It could even have cost him his life.

A habit of tearing open the bins isn't easy to kick, although it's by no means impossible with a bit of patience and consistency. Once a dog has a taste for the bins, ripping them up tends to be so enjoyable that it becomes a self-rewarding behaviour. Dogs don't even need to find a tasty snack in there to feel like they've won something; the very act of hunting and dissecting the discarded rubbish is enjoyable enough. It's like enjoying the drive so much that it doesn't matter where you're headed. The fun was in the journey.

If you plan to tackle this issue, be prepared for a journey that will last several months and require permanent changes to your routine. Every time your dog gets to trash the bin, it reinforces the behaviour and strengthens the habit. The most important starting point is to prevent the dog from doing this in the first place.

Control the environment by limiting access to the bin. Consider using a pen or a crate to stop your dog from roaming free in the kitchen when you're not home, or when it's left unattended. If it can't reach the bin, it can't destroy its contents.

Think about getting into a good routine of taking the rubbish out before leaving your dog alone. That way, if your dog manages to escape the pen and get to the bin, the worst outcome is that it'll be tipped over. There won't be a load of rubbish strewn all over the place, and it will be a bit boring for your dog, as there's nothing to enjoy ripping up.*

It may take several months for the temptation to subside. We're working on changing the value of the behaviour here, so the bin needs to become boring so it fades into the background

---

* Be aware that knocking over the bin might become the new game. If this is the case, repeat the same steps laid out here but secure the bin so that the dog can't find joy in tipping it over any more.

of the dog's worldview – a bit like that game you used to play obsessively as a kid, but then got fed up with after a while. We need to make the bin *that* game.

While it might be tempting to give your dog something even more fun to do, like leaving it with a chew or rewarding it for ignoring the bin, that isn't going to change the bin's baseline value. It might work in the short term, but it won't stop the bin from being tempting.

Remember, dogs learn associatively by making links with things that happen. They have the reasoning power of a two- to three-year-old child. It's like telling a child not to take a piece of cake off the table, and rewarding them with a toy they really want. It doesn't stop the cake from being tempting; the child only leaves it because the toy is more tempting at that moment. If the toy weren't an option, they'd likely cave in and take the cake. We want to eradicate the temptation of the bin altogether to have the best chance of changing our dogs' behaviour.

The value of something is subjective. Therefore, changing the value of something has to be done by those perceiving the value – in this case, our dogs – rather than by us imposing it. If you sat on a comfy-looking chair and it was uncomfortable, you'd move to another one. No one told you it was uncomfortable. You experienced it for yourself, liked it less and altered your behaviour by changing chairs.

Once a month, strategically set up a chance for your dog to investigate the bin. But before you do, make the bin as unattractive as possible. Take out the rubbish and spray the inside of the bin with something your dog won't like. Cider vinegar is a good option, as is citronella; either way, give your bin a good clean. The idea is that your dog will try the bin, but instead of goodness and yummy bin juice, it smells unappealing. Your dog has a go, finds it a bit unpleasant, and leaves it alone.

Consistency is vital in this case. You need to ensure your dog doesn't have a chance to fail – as soon as it does, it will increase the value of the bin, and your hard work will be undone.

Some dogs are so deeply ingrained in the habit of bin hunting that they might need more creative ways of dealing with their unhelpful behaviours. Ralph might well be one of these dogs. Notice how falling awkwardly, despite being deeply unpleasant, didn't deter him from continuing his quest.

If, after trying these steps, your dog still keeps going for the bin, work with a reputable trainer who can help you with a behavioural change programme tailored specifically to your dog. The act of trashing the bin might hold some serious intrinsic value, and you will need to find a creative way to find a learning outcome that will deter the dog. If you follow the advice in this chapter, you will have laid solid foundations, which will help your trainer get to the root of the issue much faster.

A final note on behalf of dogs everywhere. A reprimand means nothing in retrospect. If you come in to find that your dog has destroyed something, please don't scold it. Dogs only link things that have occurred within a second or so of them doing it. Because the action happened much earlier, they have nothing to link the scolding to, so they have no idea why you're angry. They just know that you're angry. Take a deep breath, scream inside your head if you need to (we're all human), clean up the mess and think about how to stop it from happening next time.

WHAT YOUR DOG IS THINKING

Summary

- Guilt is a complex emotion that dogs are unlikely to have the brain machinery to experience in the same way as humans.
- Dogs' 'guilty looks' are not a sign that they know they have done wrong; rather, dogs use submissive behaviours to calm their angry owner and show they're not a threat.
- Dogs' 'guilty looks' are often triggered in response to a scolding from their owners.
- We humans tend to look at the world through the lens of our own emotional experiences, even when we're looking at things from our dog's point of view.
- People prone to guilt are more likely to think their dog is guilty.
- People experience similar guilt over their responsibilities interfering with time spent with their dog as they do with their children.
- To stop your dog from ripping open the bin, you need to change the bin's value from your dog's perspective. This takes patience and consistency over a matter of months.
- First, change the environment to prevent your dog from accessing the bin. Use a pen or crate and regularly take the rubbish out so there is nothing there to tempt the dog.
- Periodically set up a chance for your dog to explore the bin when it's been emptied and sprayed with something your dog won't like the smell of.
- Remember not to scold your dog for a retrospective misdemeanour.

Chapter 9

What your dog is thinking about its dog friends

One reason dogs and people get along so well is that both are social creatures. For tens of thousands of years, we've lived not just side by side but together – in integrated social groups – in villages, tribes and families. We don't just thrive next to each other, minding our own business; instead, we bond closely. We become integral to each other's group, be it family or pack.

But how close are we? We're both social beings, but are we so close that we could thrive on each other's company alone? Could we ditch people altogether and just hang out with our dogs? While some of us might be nodding our heads enthusiastically and erupting into rapturous applause (this book's authors included), most people would still want some form of human company, whether a romantic partner, companion or friend. A dog is many things to us, but perhaps not absolutely everything.

What about the other way around? Do dogs cope just fine without the company of other dogs? Are we enough for them on our own? Or do they need other dog friends, too? It's a reasonable question, given that nearly seven out of ten dog owners only have one dog.[1]

Many dog owners assume their dogs need to socialise with other dogs in order for them to be well rounded and well adjusted. Rick believed this, too. He had a fox-red Labrador called Mick. Rick was an accidental Simply Red fan, having had flame-red auburn hair and acne when he was in high school; the other kids took to calling him

'Pimply Red'. Rather than taking their unkindness as the insult it was intended to be, he thought it would be ironic to start listening to Simply Red's songs. It couldn't be a slight if he actually quite liked it, and he – inadvertently – became quite the super-fan.

Rick, now in his early forties, worked in marketing and lived alone in a small new-build home in Coventry. After lockdown, the firm he worked for decided to close its physical offices permanently to save money, as remote working had worked so well for them during the pandemic. Rick liked the flexibility of remote work, but he really missed being around people. He didn't get quite the same buzz from interacting online.

To try and ease his loneliness – and to take advantage of being at home all day – he did what 3.2 million Brits did during Covid. He bought himself a puppy. A gorgeous, bouncy, joyous Labrador puppy. That's how Rick got Mick. He was so beautiful. His fur was fox red, and Rick fell in love with him immediately. You could say he was like a new flame, brightening up Rick's life.

Because Rick felt a little lonely, he wanted to give Mick the opposite experience. He had heard how important it was to 'socialise' a dog, so he started the pup off young. He took him to 'puppy parties' where basically a load of young dogs would pile in a room together and wreak utter havoc. It was an hour spent in about as much serenity as a street market in Marrakesh. It was chaos.

Mick would charge around, flinging himself at other puppies. Some would respond in kind, many would look overwhelmed, and the odd one or two would retreat under a chair and look positively shellshocked for the full hour.

There was an awkward-looking Whippet who was so overstimulated she performed what can only be described as a tail-tucked zoomie, manically dashing around but with her tail between her legs because she was nervous rather than excited. Mick saw this as an invitation to play and chased her for nearly fifteen minutes straight. Rick and the other owner thought it was hilarious, not realising that only one of the participants was actually enjoying it. The Whippet learned to avoid other dogs for fear of being harassed, and Mick learned that manners weren't necessary when it came to playing with other dogs.

Rick thought Mick was doing well, and he continued exposing him to other dogs as often as he could. There was a 'dog park' near his house, which was a well-fenced and gated area where dogs were permitted to be off-lead. It was a popular spot with dog owners, and Rick would take Mick there every day at 5.20 p.m., just after he had finished his last call for the day.

Mick loved the dog park, predominantly because it was anarchy: like a puppy party on steroids. He knew he could charge over to any dog he wanted and play – whether the other dog wanted to or not. And because people aren't generally that skilled at recognising the subtle behavioural differences between anxious and excited dogs, their owners often let bad interactions play out.

Mick was terrible for this. He was a typical giddy young Labrador, and he would run over to every dog he saw, wagging his tail exuberantly, hoping to make a new playmate. One time, he did this with a less-than-friendly German Shepherd, whose owner had responsibly kept it on a lead. Mick was running around, off-lead, sniffing the musty trail of a long-gone squirrel when the other dog caught his eye. He paused, head turned in the direction of the German Shepherd, tongue out, panting.

Mick's tail began to wag, and he took up a bold stance, almost like he was squaring up ready for a sparring match with a worthy partner. The other dog stood firmly, tail wagging quickly and aggressively, pointing straight up to the sky. This wasn't a friendly wag; this was a 'come a bit closer and find out, pal' kind of wag. Mick didn't care, and Rick didn't recognise the signs.

Undeterred by the message, Mick bounded over to the other dog, greeting him with a sniff and a play bounce. He bowed down with his front paws outstretched on the ground, his bum in the air, like a yoga downward dog. The German Shepherd started to growl. Its owner called to Rick, 'Can you get your dog, please? Mine's not friendly!'

'Sorry!' yelled Rick, as he desperately tried to recall Mick who completely blanked him. 'Mick! Mick! Come! Mick! Oh for fuck's sake . . . I'm so sorry!' he shouted, picking up the pace and jogging over in order to physically remove his dog.

Meanwhile, Mick ignored every sign of hostility, and continued to try and engage the other dog, wagging his tail more frantically and giving a sharp nose butt as if to say, 'Come on – let's play anyway!'

That was the last straw for the German Shepherd, who pounced on Mick, slamming his heavy paws on his red shoulders while attempting to lock his jaws around the soft underside of his neck. Mick squealed in pain as the other dog landed his bites, simultaneously trying to fight back.

Rick panicked and tried to grab Mick's collar, nearly losing a finger in the process. 'Shit! Shit! Mick!' he yelled as he tried to separate the dogs as they circled around the other owner, spinning on the axis of the German Shepherd's lead.

After what felt like a very long few minutes of trying, they managed to separate the two dogs, and Rick put Mick back on the lead and dragged him away. 'Your dog is vicious!' he said to the other owner.

'He's not vicious, he's a bloody dog. I told you to call your dog away, but you couldn't. Your recall is shit, and he shouldn't be off-lead if you can't get him back when you need to the most. Besides, your dog approached mine, and mine's on the lead and under control. You're the one with the problem dog, not me. Sort your dog out, mate!'

If there's one thing about dog owners, they find it difficult to take criticism about their own dogs. It's a bit like a parent being told their golden child is a bit feral. Even though we might know it to be true, we'll argue it to the death in the moment. Rick was no exception, but he came away wondering if the other owner had a point. Mick does tend to ignore him if he's interested in something else, especially if it's another dog. He was lucky this time – he just had a few scratches on his face – but it could have been much worse.

On their way back home, Rick reflected on what had happened. Besides the puppy parties for 'socialisation', he hadn't trained much with Mick. Other than 'sit' and 'paw', he only really took him for walks and called his name to get his attention, thinking that was all he needed to do. He couldn't help thinking that maybe he'd been a bit blasé, assuming the dog would know what to do, naturally. He tended to take a similar approach in work, delegating things to others without giving much time or thought to the 'how'. Stuff just got done. But the same wasn't true when it came to training his dog.

Rick wasn't sure why dogs needed to be socialised; it was just something that he'd heard so often that he took it as read. He liked watching Mick play because he looked happy when he did. And Mick being happy made him feel happy – that warm kind of 'glad' that you feel in your tummy.

The purpose of play

There are numerous theories about why dogs play.[2] It could be as simple as a response to excess energy – like a child who's eaten too many sweets and starts running around the playground. Mick certainly burned off a lot of energy at the dog park. He would gleefully run from dog to dog and was pretty much exhausted by the end of the session.

As well as burning off that excess energy, play is an important way for dogs to continually develop and hone their motor skills, which are important for hunting, fighting and social interactions. Each repetition builds muscle memory, like a dancer rehearsing their steps so often that each move becomes automatic to the beat of the music. Play activities such as chasing, biting and even wrestling all help dogs improve their coordination and strengthen muscles, improving physical fitness. Play is basically a dog gym.

Play also helps dogs train for the unexpected. When they play and turn and twist, they inevitably lose – but then regain – control over their bodies. They learn they can deal with unexpected events, not only physically but also in a confidence-building sense. They learn they can cope with failure and recover.

Play strengthens the bond between playmates, be those other dogs or people. Play is crucially important in building social cohesion. It provides an opportunity for dogs to communicate clearly. Telling each other off when things get too rough helps them learn what an acceptable interaction looks like, which can lessen the chance of future conflict. It's a bit like fighting with a sibling, which teaches you just how far you can push it before you end up in deep water.

Choosing the right playmate for your dog is really important. They're not just a buddy, they're a teacher and training partner as well. The trouble with letting your dog play with any and every other dog it comes across is that you don't know what unhelpful lessons it might be learning or what bad habits the other dog might be practising.

This also brings up the question of whether it really matters to dogs who, or what, they play with. Is a person the same as a dog or a ball? Understanding this could help us to work out what good socialisation for dogs really looks like. Dr Nicola Rooney, then a researcher at the Anthrozoology Institute at the University of Southampton, and her collaborators wanted to unearth what motivates dogs to choose a playmate and whether they might get something different from us than from other dogs.[3]

The team went to popular dog walking spots and watched people and their dogs to see how they played. They saw more than two hundred dog owners walking their dogs. Some had only one dog, others were walking several dogs.

They noticed that when people were walking multiple dogs – despite the dogs having each other to play with – they still played with their humans as much as the dogs being walked on their own.

There wasn't any evidence that dogs would play with humans less when they had another dog available to them.

It could well be that people with more than one dog are just really into their dogs and so play with them more for that reason. But a follow-on survey of more than 2,500 people found the same thing. Dogs living in homes with other dogs still played with humans as much as dogs that just lived with their owners.

It seemed that having access to another dog didn't diminish their desire to play with a human. If the motivation to play with dogs and humans were the same, you'd think they would play with the other dog because they're more accessible, and then they'd have their fill. That wasn't the case – they seemed to get something very different from playing with a person.

The same group of researchers finished up with an experiment using dogs that had only ever lived with other dogs to see if they could find any learned differences. Because the dogs all lived in a kennel, it was easier to ensure that they'd all had similar experiences previously. The experiment wouldn't have been possible had it included pet dogs that had lived with people.

The dogs were let out of their kennels and allowed to play freely with either another dog or a human. Then, a tug toy was thrown into the enclosure. The dog would grab it, and the experimenters watched to see who would take it to start a game.

In general, the dogs were more likely to instigate play with a human than a dog. When they did play with humans, they interacted more and were more likely to give up their toys to their playmates. When they played with another dog, they were more competitive than they were with a human, and wanted to win more.

In some respects, this makes sense because dogs depend on humans for resources – even those in kennels rather than in a home – as humans come and feed them. Being less competitive with people is better for their relationship – they're less likely to annoy them or damage the bond.

Whatever the reason dogs choose to play with humans over other dogs, they clearly get something different from playing with us. They seem to value interacting with us more than each other, so it's important we put the time in with our dogs to satisfy that need.

Rick spent a lot of time with Mick, given he was working from home all day, every day. But it wasn't necessarily the right kind of time. It was more like they were co-existing rather than interacting because Rick was on calls most of the day. Mick just kind of hung out with him while he did it.

That meant Mick was getting most of his 'play' time at the dog park when they went on their 5.20 p.m. walk. But the unregulated access to other dogs brought its own set of problems. Mick's recall was getting worse. Rick's calls were so often ignored that the words started losing their meaning. 'Mick, come!' no longer meant 'I should go straight to Dad': it just faded into the background because it wasn't paired with anything meaningful. All Mick heard was noise, while he was getting on with paying attention to whatever game he was playing at the time. It's a bit like living next to a busy road. When you first move in, you notice the traffic noise, but after a while it blurs into the background. You become *habituated* to it. Mick had become habituated to Rick's recall command.

The other issue with this kind of approach to socialisation is that Mick would get so used to free play with other dogs at the park that he began to expect free play with all the dogs he came across. Rick found he started pulling on the lead uncontrollably when he saw another dog, trying to get to it to play. And whenever he was a street away from the dog park, Mick would basically drag Rick down the road, pulling so hard he was wheezing as his collar cut off his airway.

Mick's poor behaviour happened because he was anticipating playing with other dogs without any rules or structure in place to guide him. Play is an important activity for dogs. It helps them develop critical behaviours like interacting and hunting through practising predatory strategies. Play is also something that all dogs do instinctively, meaning that there must be some common biological underpinnings.

This makes sense from an evolutionary perspective too. Dogs who were more likely to play with people were more likely to appeal to humans and be socialised into human groups. They thrived more from access to our food and they reproduced more. Those traits were naturally selected and bred into subsequent generations.

A group of researchers in Chile and the USA led by Alejandra Rossi analysed blood samples from dogs immediately after they played to measure levels of key hormones that might play a part in their behaviours, like cortisol and oxytocin.[4] Remember, cortisol is released when dogs (or people) experience something stressful. It prepares the body for the interaction by increasing energy levels available in the short term and getting the muscles ready to work. Oxytocin, on the other hand, is a brain chemical involved in social bonding, love and trust. These are all potentially important factors when thinking about the social aspects of play.

The scientists were interested in the relationships between hormonal levels and their observed play behaviours. They found that lower cortisol levels were linked with longer bouts of play and exploration. This makes sense, as dogs – like us – are more likely to play and explore when they're less stressed. Lower cortisol levels reflect a state of lower anxiety, making dogs more open to new environments and social interactions.

The link with oxytocin was slightly less clear cut, but in 2015, Theresa Romero, from Kyoto University in Japan, led a group of researchers to shed more light on its role in play.[5] Knowing that the hormone is involved in social behaviours, like pair-bonding and mother–infant bonding, they figured it was likely that it could also have a role in other social behaviours, like play.

In their experiment, sixteen dogs were given either a squirt of oxytocin or a placebo spray up the nose and then put in a room with their owners and another dog that they already knew. The other dog and the human would be their 'playmates'. Dogs that had been given oxytocin played more and for longer. They also gave signals that they wanted to play, like play-bows, more often than the dogs who had the placebo. This was true of playing with both the other dog and the human.

Oxytocin made dogs more playful, acting like a volume switch – as the volume (or oxytocin) went up, it made them want to play more. Mick had an oxytocin and adrenaline boost when he wanted to play with other dogs, but had absolutely no manners. This was a recipe for disaster, driving more and more interactions that were not constructive for him.

In truth, Mick would have got just as much from Rick, if Rick had focused on quality interactions with him. He didn't really need to play with any other dog he met. He would have received the same benefits from spending quality time with Rick, both from a social and enrichment perspective.

It is OK for your dog to want to play with other dogs; it's not that they *should* only play with their human companions. But they don't necessarily *need* to be friends with every dog they encounter. And if, like Mick, they get so overwhelmingly excited by the sight of other dogs in anticipation of playing with them, then it's definitely a problem. It means they will likely stop listening to their owner in favour of seeking out the thrill of a game of chase or a play fight with another dog. It's at this point that people think their dog isn't listening or is just plain stubborn, but the reality is that the dog is not psychologically in a place where it can retain lessons because it's so aroused. It's like telling a child they're going to Disneyland and then giving them homework to do and being surprised when they can't concentrate. Dogs can't concentrate in a state of over-arousal either.

Remember, canine chaos might be fun, but it's not socialisation. Not in the way your dog needs it, anyway. Consider socialisation as gentle exposure to things your dog might find exciting, be scared of or feel like it needs to challenge. Instead of the 'social' aspect of sociali-sation being about interactions and play time, consider it to be about teaching your dog how to cope with all the things it's likely to cross paths with. It's about promoting healthy behaviours rather than making friends. When a dog is exposed to these things, and you teach it how to respond, it can build powerful habits that are internalised as coping strategies, creating a well-balanced, happy and stable dog.

Try this: Proper dog socialisation – impulse control 101
Before we start, take everything you've heard previously about socialising your dog, put it in the bin and follow these steps instead. Socialising your dog properly has nothing to do with going to the dog park, getting your dog to make friends with all your mates' dogs or encouraging unsolicited bouts of zoomies with the Collie from two roads down.

Your dog's socialisation begins in a distraction-free environment, like your garden or even your living room. We will begin by teaching your dog that it's highly valuable for it to look at you. The aim is to build strong foundations for engagement. This will help you significantly later on when your dog is being 'socialised' in the world with things it might find distracting.

Have some really high-value treats at the ready – something your dog absolutely loves, like cheese or bits of cooked meat. This will be important as we progress because your dog needs to be certain that the engagement we're about to teach is absolutely worth its while. Different dogs will prefer a different currency of 'payment'. Some might prefer food, treating it as high value, others might prefer a toy, while some might value your praise and interaction above all else.

Walk around, let your dog sniff or go about its business. Don't make a sound or try and get its attention, but as soon as it looks at you, give it a reward. You can use your *bridge command,* like 'yes', to signal that a reward is coming if you like (see Chapter 1). The idea is that your dog figures out that looking at you triggers a very high-value reward. This is called 'shaping' the behaviour.

Once your dog has clearly established that concept, you can progress to doing the same thing in a slightly more distracting environment. Remember, patience is important so build this up slowly. Try repeating the same exercise outside the front of your house. It's familiar, but not overwhelming. Walk a few paces to the left and then turn around and walk a few paces to the right, continually watching for your dog to look at you and then rewarding it. Be subtle – remember, you're rewarding it for choosing to disengage with something in its environment and looking at you, not bribing it to look at you with a visual signal.

It's important that you reward your dog every single time you get the behaviour you want. This is an impressionable time in its training. It needs to know with certainty that it will get paid, or you might be left with an inconsistent result and intermittent behaviour.

It's also worth being mindful of the number of calories your dog will have when you're teaching this. You might want to consider slightly reducing its usual food intake, being mindful that it maintains a balanced diet and you don't inadvertently cause it to put on weight. Don't worry, you won't need to do this forever. You just need to spend some time conditioning the behaviour and, in time, it will become self-rewarding without the need for treats.

Once your dog has built a strong response, you can start to increase the distractions. This time, you could introduce a 'stooge' dog. Get a friend with a dog to come along and do the same thing from a distance. Wait it out – don't try and distract your dog – but as soon as it disengages its attention from the other dog and looks at you, mark it with a 'yes' and reward it. If you don't know anyone with a dog, you could do this every time you go for a walk and come across another dog, but make sure you keep your distance to begin with. Get closer to the distraction gradually, over several sessions. Remember, slow incremental increases in difficulty will get you the best results. Be patient!

Be selective; if the other dog is too excitable or aroused it might be too much for your dog at this early point. If you struggle, any good and reputable trainer should have a selection of well-behaved dogs you could work with.

Once you're happy with your dog's progress at this stage, look to make the distraction even more distracting. If it's a stooge dog, get the owner to play with it, or play with a ball, and every time your dog chooses to look at you, mark and reward.

As your dog becomes proficient, you can start looking for opportunities to do this on walks. If your dog sees a squirrel or a cat, for example, but looks at you, mark and reward. If it doesn't look at you, or pays too much interest and takes too long, don't worry. Don't distract it; instead, change direction then walk back and repeat the exercise until it does look at you, then mark and reward.

If you notice that there is a particular distraction that your dog will not ignore or a distance that you can't quite get past, then you're ready to move on to the last stage. This is to overlay a consequence for non-compliance. It's important that we teach our dog that it's super-rewarding to come back to us, and that ignoring us is non-negotiable.

This time, when your dog ignores the recall, give a firm pop on the lead to interrupt it (again, don't pull your dog towards you: the aim is to interrupt the hyper-fixation on the distraction). If the previous steps have been followed, your dog should default to look at you. When this happens, mark with a 'yes', run backwards so your dog is encouraged to enthusiastically return to you, and reward when it gets to you. There's no need to make it sit or anything else: just reward it for coming back, and walk on.* Then proof-test that particular distraction by repeating it, making it more and more challenging by moving closer to the dog's threshold – always ensuring it succeeds before you increase the difficulty. You should notice that things you previously had to 'pop' for start to reduce. This is a sign of progression. Remember, like people, dogs can make mistakes. Relapse is a healthy part of behavioural change and gives the opportunity to strengthen previous gaps.

Next, you'll mix in the foundations of recall (see Chapter 2). Only this time, start the dog on its lead, using a few paces of slack. Recall it when it's at a distance from the distraction and then pay it when it disengages and comes to you. This is why you need to establish the behaviour using a high-value reward – it's got to be worth the dog coming back for. Then, progress to doing this on a long line (even if it has great recall, so it doesn't have the option to fail). Build up the levels of distraction and practise in various places so the behaviour becomes generalised. Build your distance slowly, gradually getting closer and closer to life's distractions, before calling your dog back.

Once you're confident, you can do this with your dog off the long lead. The whole point is to make sure your dog will always choose you over anything that might be interesting or distracting, including another dog that might want to play. Make it unpredictable – call it back randomly whenever you're out and about, then send it back off for more free play. This ensures it doesn't inadvertently have a precursor that signals

---

* A common mistake is to make your dog sit on its return and then reward it. By doing this, you are inadvertently rewarding the sit, instead of being clear about the behaviour you want and reinforcing it to come back to you.

what you're about to do and increases the likelihood that it will always focus on you above anything else around. And if you have any doubt about whether your dog will find something a bit too tempting and might ignore you, call it back sooner. Prevention is much better than cure.

Remember, the key to this is consistency and repetition. You're building this to be an automatic response that your dog no longer needs to think about, and this takes time to condition. Think of it as a kind of muscle memory. If you were set a challenge to get five basketballs in a hoop in a row, you might get the odd one initially, but there would be more misses than scores. After time and practice you will score more consistently, and eventually you'll get the shot every time. Individual talent matters – some might be naturally better than others and need less practice, but all will get there eventually. So be patient with your dog and keep up the repetitions until it's an automatic response.

Now a brief point about multi-dog households. If you have more than one dog, limit the time they have for free and unstructured play together. Ration their zoomies and make time to train each dog separately, or the temptation to play with each other might undermine your ability to establish the ground rules.

Finally, rest easy, because your dog doesn't necessarily have to have a dog-on-dog play ban. But do use your common sense. Many dogs will be fine having some free play time with dogs that you know and trust and with which you can ensure a good relationship. Be aware of any signs that your dog has an unhealthy interest in prioritising other dogs. For example, if it barks, whines or pulls even at a distance when it sees another dog, that's a sign that you need to focus on building in quality human–dog time rather than flooding it with excitement by letting it play with other dogs.

If you allow your dog to play with other dogs, be aware that fights can break out in a fraction of a second. It might be normal dog behaviour and, to an extent, it is how dogs reprimand each other, but it can get out of hand, especially if one dog isn't taking the hint and continues to pester or aggravate the other. Either way, dog fights can be alarming and result in one or both parties sustaining an injury. Understand that dogs can play rough, but stay vigilant and remove your dog if there are clear signs of escalation by putting it on a lead and walking away.

Summary
- Dogs play for several reasons: to burn off excess energy, to practise behaviours like those used for hunting, and to learn how to interact socially with others.
- Dogs have different motivations for playing with humans and with other dogs.
- Dogs are hardwired to play – hormones like cortisol and oxytocin affect how much a dog plays.
- Good socialisation for dogs means exposing them to things they might find distracting and teaching them how to respond healthily. Uncontrolled play with other dogs can lead to bad habits and dogs being over-aroused in anticipation when they see other dogs.
- Teach your dog to engage with you in exchange for a high-value reward.
- Move on to rewarding your dog near distractions when it disengages and looks at you instead.
- Build up the levels of distraction and practise in a range of places to generalise the behaviour.
- Mix in recalling your dog in the presence of distractions, starting small and building up the difficulty levels.

Afterword

Dogs are incredible. They have evolved alongside humans and, as such, have changed biologically and neurologically in ways that help them thrive with us. Their brains have developed special parts to process human voices, and they are super-sensitive to our emotions. They can elicit how we feel from our voices, are highly attuned to human faces, and catch our yawns in a way that even the great apes can't.

We wrote this book because dogs needed us to write it, and they needed their humans to read it. All of us will, at times, have mistaken our dog's intentions, communications or thoughts – because we're examining the situation through our own human eyes. And that means we can get it wrong and respond in a way that confuses or upsets our dogs at best and, at worst, can make problem behaviours even worse. We hope that reading this book has helped you to step back and see things through your dog's eyes as well.

That's not to say, however, we should ignore a human perspective altogether. Our dogs rely on us to show them how to thrive in a human world – whether taking a lead from us through social referencing, smelling our mood through the chemosignals we emit, or learning from us when it comes to coping with scary things. We need to interpret situations and then translate them into dog language so we can communicate what we need our dogs to do, and understand them when they communicate their needs to us.

One thing is for certain: many of us have incredibly close bonds with our dogs. It's possible to bond with a dog as strongly as you would with another person. We commonly refer to ourselves as mum or dad to our dogs, and there is some support grounded in science for that approach, given that the same brain patterns are activated when mothers look at either their children or their dogs. We see dogs as family. Humans and dogs have the same brain chemicals that allow them to bond with and trust each other and, dare we say, even love each other.

Sometimes, though, we love our dogs so much that we inadvertently make things harder for them. We try hard to ensure they're always happy and having fun because that's what we want for anyone we love. But by doing this, we don't teach them how to cope in an inevitably stressful world. Stress can greatly impact our dogs, even shortening their lifespan.

It's impossible to eliminate all the things that make our dogs nervous – and for some, this can be something as innocuous as seeing another dog, or the noise of normal traffic. They rely on us to help them navigate their everyday environment. Rather than avoiding stressful experiences altogether in favour of a lovely, happy, sheltered experience, our dogs need us to help them build resilience so that the things that were once anxiety-provoking just fade into the background.

It's precisely because we're so close to our dogs that we sometimes doubt ourselves as owners. We wonder whether we're doing the right things for them, especially if our dogs are doing things that we don't like, or that are dangerous, and which we don't know how to deal with. Such behaviours include, for example, barking and lunging at other dogs, ignoring us when we call them back, or – heaven forbid – tearing up the kitchen bin bag. Sometimes, we feel embarrassed and think people judge us for things our dogs do, even if it's something we can't help, such as their anxiety making them react in a certain way. At times, we end up getting frustrated. But our dogs don't understand we're cross about something they've done – they think we're cross with them, and that makes them uncomfortable and worried. And then we feel bad and, usually, very, very guilty.

We hope that our insights from the hundreds of research studies in these pages help bridge the gap between the human and canine mind so you can more clearly understand what your dog is thinking, especially when it's behaving in a way that's difficult for you to deal with. The science we've laid out links to some practical ways you can change the dynamic between you and your dog and, undoubtedly, improve their behaviour too.

But remember: just like people, dogs are individuals. There are many, many ways to train them or address a particular behaviour. While we were discussing, researching and analysing this book, Dr Sab noticed little quirks and differences in how her three dogs learn, in exactly the way Danny talked about. Luther is driven by the chance to play and interact with her, whereas Red will do anything at all for food. And Jimmy . . . well, he just wants a quiet life sitting on any available lap.

Not every problem can be solved with treats alone. This approach might work initially until your dog is more motivated by something else – like chasing that cat rather than coming when called. Imagine you're speeding, and rather than stopping you and giving you a fine, the police wait for you to slow down and then give you £200 for doing the right thing. Getting £200 at random intervals for behaving properly would be really motivating most of the time . . . until that one time when you're late for a job interview and getting there fast becomes the more appealing option. The ideas we've set out here will help you build solid foundations with your dog, where the motivation to behave in a certain way becomes intrinsic – without the need for anything external like treats.

If your dog does something you wish it didn't for long enough, that something becomes a habit. And quitting a habit can be tough, even when you want to. Anyone who's ever tried to stop biting their nails will attest to that. Despite being able to rationalise why it's bad for you and that it hurts, stopping it is a tricky task. No lotion, potion or magic piece of equipment will fix it. Many people who come through

Danny's doors have already spent a fortune trying various fixes and training methodologies based on promises that didn't materialise into practice. The reality is that you need to have a completely dog-centred strategy tailored to your individual dog. It will take patience and perseverance. Lasting change always takes time.

The science-backed strategies in this book will help you establish good foundations for your training and tackle various behavioural problems. But if you need more help and are looking for a reputable trainer, make sure you can see cases where they've successfully worked with dogs with similar issues. Academic qualifications don't automatically translate into practical skills, and years of experience don't always mean someone has gained the knowledge to grow. One thing's for certain: dogs don't lie. Let their visible results be your recommendation.

Danny's attitude to training has always been based on an individual approach to dogs. He takes the theory about how dogs learn and applies it to the dog in front of him, thinking critically and tweaking his approach as he goes.

Working with Dr Sab to unpack the science has confirmed what he knew to be true from his practical experience, with many 'Eureka!' moments along the way! For example, when we talked about whether dogs could feel guilt, the neuroscience backed up exactly what Danny had always thought. Dogs don't have the brain structure to experience guilt – they were responding submissively to avoid a telling off! On the other hand, Dr Sab has been equally amazed at how our common beliefs about how dogs think differ so much from the actual science. Despite drowning in information about dogs, we're often left starving for wisdom. This book will help dog owners navigate the conflicting information and common misconceptions about dogs to improve their behaviour.

One final, final thing. The quality of time you invest in your dog is much more important than the quantity of time you spend with it. So always be present when you're with your dog. Stop scrolling, put down your phone . . . and enjoy that incredible bond.

Acknowledgements

Sometimes we get so fixated on the destination that we forget to enjoy the journey. With some degree of certainty, we can both say that the journey of writing this book was a scream. We spent hours discussing the science and dog stories on Zoom calls every week – usually on Monday night. However, Dr Sab would often press the turbo button and make us do it twice a week if we were running behind. (By running behind, she meant anything that wasn't two chapters ahead of schedule!)

Since we both have busy day jobs, our Zooms inevitably meant multi-tasking. We've held them when we're with the dogs (obviously), preparing food, sitting in car parks after going to the shops, and even on holiday by the side of the pool (a deadline is a deadline). Dr Sab often travels for work and research, and pages have been written in five continents and ten countries, with poor Danny suffering the time zone differences.

But we got there! And we're glad you're here with us at the end of this book!

One of the really special things about this journey has been the chance to go on it with a friend. There was much love and mutual respect during this process, driven by what's become a deeply soulful friendship. Although we came into this project with very different sets of expertise, we were definitely on the same wavelength throughout. We would regularly say the same things simultaneously and erupt into fits of laughter while shouting, 'We've done it again!' And we don't mean once or twice. This happened all the time. Often when

Dr Sab drafted something and read it back to Danny, he would stop her and say, 'We should add X or talk about Y', and the next paragraph would already cover the exact same thing. It was spooky how the universe had smooshed us together – from very different angles – and yet how similarly we were thinking.

Although we had a lot of fun writing this book, it was no easy journey. But anything worth doing – and we mean *really* worth doing – is hard. It requires you to roll your sleeves up and push through something tough. At this point (*Dr Sab here*), I want to talk about how proud I am of Danny. He has severe ADHD, so by its very nature the writing process is the antithesis of how he would prefer to function with his traits. One of which is *waiting mode*. For someone with ADHD, having any scheduled appointment renders you in waiting mode for the entire day, until said appointment is done. Even scheduling a meeting was challenging, with Dr Sab sending regular reminders and signing them off 'from your PA x'. But still, Danny pushed through and showed up week after week, putting in hours and hours of research and writing.

Then there was the sitting down and focusing for hours at a time. ADHD is often misunderstood. It's not that you can't focus on anything – it's more that you focus on everything. Because of this, Danny would actually pay attention to more things than most people. But he couldn't turn down the background noise to concentrate on something in front of him that was important. So he found new strategies. He would lean his phone up against anything (depending on where he was) and pace around the room when his concentration was dipping. At times I would just catch repeated glimpses of his torso, constantly passing by the camera like a drive-by. Until, that is, he had something important to contribute, and he would run towards the camera excitedly, like a child racing to get the last ice cream. I'd get a close-up of his seemingly giant head, accompanied by a loud, distorted voice. Sometimes, the phone would slip down, and I'd be left with a view of the ceiling, or Danny would disappear into the abyss as it landed face down, and I'd have to shout for ages before he would notice it. (On the plus side, he'd usually get over twenty-five thousand steps in on book nights.)

Danny worked relentlessly to overcome the challenges that ADHD presented and has definitely grown as a result. I know just how hard and all-consuming it was to write this book. I have an unwavering adoration for Danny's strength and tenacity to see it through, and he worked to an impeccable standard. And on top of that, he had me pushing him to work harder and faster so we could stay ahead of schedule.

In addition, he is one of the humblest people you could meet. He didn't find it easy to take credit for his many achievements, which were fundamental to our having the content we needed for this book. I, however, am very happy to shout about them on his behalf.

Danny here. Now it's my turn to say thanks to Dr Sab. It's not often you find someone with such an open mind to see past the deeply ingrained myths and misconceptions that have become so commonplace in relation to dogs. I'm grateful that you could. You approached the science with forensic precision, unravelling each analysis with clarity and thoughtfulness to extract the evidence we needed to inform our long and enthusiastic discussions about the implications for dogs and their owners. And challenging long-held beliefs isn't easy – as any of us who've tried to explain that a dog doesn't actually feel guilty to a dog-lover can attest to. Thank you for standing side by side with me as we do this in this book . . . without ducking for cover.

It's also remarkable that you have a high workload and have still found a way to make it all come together. Not least because you would always work around my somewhat inflexible schedule as a small business owner. I really appreciate you for that.

We also have some 'thank yous' to say to those who have been fundamental in making this book a reality. The first goes to the dogs in our lives – every dog we have ever had – especially Brodie and Luther, who are the origin story of this book and the pair that made the universe smoosh us together. Out of you both, everything has grown, and we're eternally grateful for that. We're also indebted to every dog we've ever worked with and researched. Every single dog has taught us something invaluable, and those lessons permeate these pages and have enabled us to share that wisdom with you.

We're grateful to every client who has ever trusted Danny with their dogs and put their faith in his Unleashed K9 methods, and to Danny's talented team of trainers: Robbie Lindsey, Connor Dickson and Simon Cooper. While spending all day, every day, playing with dogs might sound like a perfect job, the reality of the cases the team works with is very different. They're constantly helping owners deal with difficult behaviours with their dogs. That can be hard – especially for the owners who have often tried everything and want to have a good relationship with their dog. They're contactable whenever needed – dogs don't just keep their problem behaviours to office hours. And that takes its toll emotionally. Thank you for your ongoing commitment and compassion that sets Unleashed K9 apart from the rest. And recently, they've really stepped up and put in extra hours to free Danny up to progress projects like this book, allowing us to reach many more people and their dogs. Gentlemen, we appreciate you.

A really special thank you goes to Jamie and Lou Penrith, whose tireless efforts campaigning for the welfare of animals make a difference to so many. Their hours of unpaid work are unseen by many, but appreciated by us all.

We are massively grateful to our brilliant editor, Tom Asker. Your belief in us and enthusiasm for this book have kept our spirits high and our noses to the grindstone! Your advice and support have helped us hugely, and it's been such a pleasure to work with you. An enormous thank you to the most brilliant publicist, Clara Diaz;

marketeer, Lucy Sharpe; cover designer, Sophie Ellis; audio lead, Jessica Callaghan, and production lead, John Fairweather.

Thank you to Matt Crossey, who helped us get the book out there into the world, and to Will Carne and all at WillCa Studios and the whole Dog Scholar team who have helped us reach people with dog science who wouldn't otherwise have thought about it.

A big thank you goes out to Professor Rob Honey, Dr Sab's collaborator at Cardiff University. Dr Sab trained under Professor Rob, and his relentless support of her research ideas has been crucial in turning plans into data. And a final nod to Harry and everyone at dog training, with whom Dr Sab and Luther have spent many a happy Saturday morning thinking about nothing but the wonder of dogs.

Not everyone is lucky enough to have the chance to sit down with one of their closest mates and do something that you both really believe in. We have been that lucky, and we really believe in this book. The chance to dust off research papers that are too often left on a shelf, extract the wisdom from hundreds of scientists, and then apply it to practical dog training to help dogs and their owners, was an absolute gift. It allowed us to be part of something bigger than ourselves, and we're incredibly grateful for that.

A final thank you must go out to you for reading this book.

Endnotes

Chapter 1

1 Horn, L., Range, F., & Huber, L. (2013). Dogs' attention towards humans depends on their relationship, not only on social familiarity. *Animal Cognition, 16*, 435–443.

2 Nagasawa, M., Mogi, K., & Kikusui, T. (2009). Attachment between humans and dogs. *Japanese Psychological Research, 51*(3), 209–221.

3 Rathish, D., Rajapakse, R. P. V. J., & Weerakoon, K. G. A. D. (2021). The role of cortisol in the association of canine-companionship with blood pressure, glucose, and lipids: A systematic review. *High Blood Pressure & Cardiovascular Prevention, 28*, 447–455.

4 Berns, G. S., Brooks, A. M., & Spivak, M. (2015). Scent of the familiar: An fMRI study of canine brain responses to familiar and unfamiliar human and dog odors. *Behavioural Processes, 110*, 37–46.

5 Cook, P. F., Prichard, A., Spivak, M., & Berns, G. S. (2016). Awake canine fMRI predicts dogs' preference for praise vs food. *Social Cognitive and Affective Neuroscience, 11*(12), 1853–1862.

6 Haruno, M., Kuroda, T., Doya, K., Toyama, K., Kimura, M., Samejima, K., & Kawato, M. (2004). A neural correlate of reward-based behavioral learning in caudate nucleus: a functional magnetic resonance imaging study of a stochastic decision task. *Journal of Neuroscience, 24*(7), 1660–1665.

7 Fisher, H. E. (1992). *Anatomy of Love – a natural history of adultery, monogamy and divorce.* Simon & Schuster Ltd. London, 54–57.

8 Odendaal, J. S., & Lehmann, S. M. C. (2000). The role of phenylethylamine during positive human–dog interaction. *Acta Veterinaria Brno, 69*(3), 183–188.

9 Nagasawa, M., Kikusui, T., Onaka, T., & Ohta, M. (2009). Dog's gaze at its owner increases owner's urinary oxytocin during social interaction. *Hormones and Behavior, 55*(3), 434–441.

10 Bosch, O. J., & Young, L. J. (2018). Oxytocin and social relationships: from attachment to bond disruption. *Behavioral Pharmacology of Neuropeptides: Oxytocin*, 97–117.

11 Ogata, N. (2016). Separation anxiety in dogs: what progress has been made in our understanding of the most common behavioral problems in dogs? *Journal of Veterinary Behavior, 16,* 28–35.

Chapter 2

1 Balsam, P. D., & Tomie, A. (1985). *Context and Learning.* Erlbaum, Hillsdale, N.J.

2 Turner, T. N., Stafford, S. G., McHugh, M. B., Surovik, L., Delgross, D., & Fad, O. (1991). The effects of context shift in killer whales (*Orcinus Orca*). In: Allen, S. (ed) *Proceedings of the International Marine Animal Trainers Association 1991 Annual Conference,* 4–8 November 1991.

3 Gibsone, S., McBride, E. A., Redhead, E. S., Cameron, K. E., & Bizo, L. A. (2021). The effectiveness of visual and auditory elements of a compound stimulus in controlling behavior in the domestic dog (Canis familiaris). *Journal of Veterinary Behavior, 46,* 87–96.

4 Herman, J. P., Figueiredo, H., Mueller, N. K., Ulrich-Lai, Y., Ostrander, M. M., Choi, D. C., & Cullinan, W. E. (2003). Central mechanisms of stress integration: hierarchical circuitry controlling hypothalamo–pituitary–adrenocortical responsiveness. *Frontiers in Neuroendocrinology, 24*(3), 151–180.

5 Starcke, K., Wiesen, C., Trotzke, P., & Brand, M. (2016). Effects of acute laboratory stress on executive functions. *Frontiers in Psychology, 7,* 461.

6 Verhage, A., Noppe, J., Feys, Y., & Ledegen, E. (2018). Force, stress, and decision-making within the Belgian police: the impact of stressful situations on police decision-making. *Journal of Police and Criminal Psychology, 33,* 345–357.

Chapter 3

1 Slabbert, J. M., & Rasa, O. A. E. (1997). Observational learning of an acquired maternal behaviour pattern by working dog pups: an alternative training method? *Applied Animal Behaviour Science, 53*(4), 309–316.

2 Merola, I., Prato-Previde, E., & Marshall-Pescini, S. (2012). Dogs' social referencing towards owners and strangers. *PLOS One, 7*(10), e47653.

3 Cook, P., Prichard, A., Spivak, M., & Berns, G. S. (2017). Awake fMRI Reveals Covert Arousal in Aggressive Dogs Under Social Resource Threat. *BioRxiv,* 203323.

4 Wan, M., Bolger, N., & Champagne, F. A. (2012). Human perception of fear in dogs varies according to experience with dogs. *PLOS One, 7*(12), e51775.

5 Kujala, M. V., Kujala, J., Carlson, S., & Hari, R. (2012). Dog experts' brains distinguish socially relevant body postures similarly in dogs and humans. *PLOS One,* 7(6), e39145.

6 D'Aniello, B., Fierro, B., Scandurra, A., Pinelli, C., Aria, M., & Semin, G. R. (2021). Sex differences in the behavioural responses of dogs exposed to human chemosignals of fear and happiness. *Animal Cognition, 24*(2), 299–309.

Chapter 4

1 Pongrácz, P., Molnár, C., & Miklósi, Á. (2010). Barking in family dogs: an ethological approach. *The Veterinary Journal, 183*(2), 141–147.

2 Molnár, C., Kaplan, F., Roy, P., Pachet, F., Pongrácz, P., Dóka, A., & Miklósi, Á. (2008). Classification of dog barks: a machine learning approach. *Animal Cognition, 11,* 389–400.

3 Andics, A., Gácsi, M., Faragó, T., Kis, A., & Miklósi, Á. (2014). Voice-sensitive regions in the dog and human brain are revealed by comparative fMRI. *Current Biology, 24*(5), 574–578.

4 https://www.youtube.com/channel/UCmcw8iczWgGnOP7sP-D70wg

5 Kaminski, J., Call, J., & Fischer, J. (2004). Word learning in a domestic dog: evidence for 'fast mapping'. *Science* (New York, N.Y.), 304(5677), 1682–1683. https://doi.org/10.1126/science.1097859

6 Andics, A., Gábor, A., Gácsi, M., Faragó, T., Szabó, D., & Miklósi, A. (2016). Neural mechanisms for lexical processing in dogs. *Science, 353*(6303), 1030–1032.

7 Bräuer, J., Kaminski, J., Riedel, J., Call, J., & Tomasello, M. (2006). Making inferences about the location of hidden food: social dog, causal ape. *Journal of Comparative Psychology, 120*(1), 38.

8 Kaminski, J., Schulz, L., & Tomasello, M. (2012). How dogs know when communication is intended for them. *Developmental Science, 15*(2), 222–232.

Chapter 5

1 Kurdek, L. A. (2008). Pet dogs as attachment figures. *Journal of Social and Personal Relationships, 25*(2), 247–266.

2 Shipman, P. (2010). The animal connection and human evolution. *Current Anthropology, 51,* 519–538.

3 Stoeckel, L. E., Palley, L. S., Gollub, R. L., Niemi, S. M., & Evins, A. E. (2014). Patterns of brain activation when mothers view their own child and dog: An fMRI study. *PLOS One,* 9(10), e107205.

4 Karl, S., Boch, M., Zamansky, A., van der Linden, D., Wagner, I. C., Völter,

C. J., & Huber, L. (2020). Exploring the dog–human relationship by combining fMRI, eye-tracking and behavioural measures. *Scientific Reports, 10*(1), 22273.

5 MacLean, E. L., Gesquiere, L. R., Gee, N. R., Levy, K., Martin, W. L., & Carter, C. S. (2017). Effects of affiliative human–animal interaction on dog salivary and plasma oxytocin and vasopressin. *Frontiers in Psychology, 8,* 1606.

6 Herbeck, Y. E., Eliava, M., Grinevich, V., & MacLean, E. L. (2022). Fear, love, and the origins of canid domestication: An oxytocin hypothesis. *Comprehensive Psychoneuroendocrinology, 9,* 100100.

7 Ruan, C., & Zhang, Z. (2016). Laboratory domestication changed the expression patterns of oxytocin and vasopressin in brains of rats and mice. *Anatomical Science International, 91,* 358–370.

8 Hori, Y., Kishi, H., Inoue-Murayama, M., & Fujita, K. (2013). Dopamine receptor D4 gene (DRD4) is associated with gazing toward humans in domestic dogs (Canis familiaris). *Open Journal of Animal Sciences, 3,* 54–58.

Chapter 6

1 Dreschel, N. A. (2010). The effects of fear and anxiety on health and lifespan in pet dogs. *Applied Animal Behaviour Science, 125*(3–4), 157–162.

2 Dale, A. R., Walker, J. K., Farnworth, M. J., Morrissey, S. V., & Waran, N. K. (2010). A survey of owners' perceptions of fear of fireworks in a sample of dogs and cats in New Zealand. *New Zealand Veterinary Journal, 58*(6), 286–291.

3 Vermeire, S., Audenaert, K., Dobbeleir, A., De Meester, R., Vandermeulen, E., Waelbers, T., & Peremans, K. (2009). Regional cerebral blood flow changes in dogs with anxiety disorders, measured with SPECT. *Brain Imaging and Behavior, 3,* 342–349.

4 Riva, J., Bondiolotti, G., Michelazzi, M., Verga, M., & Carenzi, C. (2008). Anxiety related behavioural disorders and neurotransmitters in dogs. *Applied Animal Behaviour Science, 114*(1–2), 168–181.

5 Mariti, C., Gazzano, A., Moore, J. L., Baragli, P., Chelli, L., & Sighieri, C. (2012). Perception of dogs' stress by their owners. *Journal of Veterinary Behavior, 7*(4), 213–219.

6 Moesta, A., Kim, G., Wilson-Frank, C. R., Weng, H. Y., & Ogata, N. (2020). Comparison of serum brain-derived neurotrophic factor in dogs with and without separation anxiety. *Journal of Veterinary Behavior, 35,* 14–18.

7 Riemer, S. (2020). Effectiveness of treatments for firework fears in dogs. *Journal of Veterinary Behavior, 37,* 61–70.

8 Otto, C. M., Downend, A. B., Serpell, J. A., Ziemer, L. S., & Saunders, H. M. (2004). Medical and behavioral surveillance of dogs deployed to the World Trade Center and the Pentagon from October 2001 to June 2002. *Journal of the American Veterinary Medical Association, 225*(6), 861–867.

Chapter 7

1 Mugford, R. A. (1987). The influence of nutrition on canine behaviour. *Journal of Small Animal Practice, 28,* 1046–1055.

2 Reisner, I. R., Mann, J. J., Stanley, M., Huang, Y. Y., & Houpt, K. A. (1996). Comparison of cerebrospinal fluid monoamine metabolite levels in dominant-aggressive and non-aggressive dogs. *Brain Research, 714*(1–2), 57–64.

3 Linnoila, M., Virkkunen, M., Scheinin, M., Nuutila, A., Rimon, R., & Goodwin, F. K. (1983). Low cerebrospinal fluid 5-hydroxyindoleacetic acid concentration differentiates impulsive from nonimpulsive violent behavior, *Life Science, 33,* 2609–2614.

4 Orwell's story is based on the case study by Suñol, A., Perez-Accino, J., Kelley, M., Rossi, G., & Schmitz, S. S. (2020). Successful dietary treatment of aggression and behavioral changes in a dog. *Journal of Veterinary Behavior, 37,* 56–60.

5 DeNapoli, J. S., Dodman, N. H., Shuster, L., Rand, W. M., & Gross, K. L. (2000). Effect of dietary protein content and tryptophan supplementation on dominance aggression, territorial aggression, and hyperactivity in dogs. *Journal of the American Veterinary Medical Association, 217*(4), 504–508.

6 Re, S., Zanoletti, M., & Emanuele, E. (2008). Aggressive dogs are characterized by low omega-3 polyunsaturated fatty acid status. *Veterinary Research Communications, 32,* 225–230.

7 Puurunen, J., Sulkama, S., Tiira, K., Araujo, C., Lehtonen, M., Hanhineva, K., & Lohi, H. (2016). A non-targeted metabolite profiling pilot study suggests that tryptophan and lipid metabolisms are linked with ADHD-like behaviours in dogs. *Behavioral and Brain Functions, 12,* 1–13.

8 Lit, L., Belanger, J. M., Boehm, D., Lybarger, N., & Oberbauer, A. M. (2013). Differences in behavior and activity associated with a poly(a) expansion in the dopamine transporter in Belgian Malinois. *PLOS One, 8*(12), e82948.

9 Packer, R. M., Law, T. H., Davies, E., Zanghi, B., Pan, Y., & Volk, H. A.

(2016). Effects of a ketogenic diet on ADHD-like behavior in dogs with idiopathic epilepsy. *Epilepsy & Behavior, 55*, 62–68.

10 Sechi, S., Di Cerbo, A., Canello, S., Guidetti, G., Chiavolelli, F., Fiore, F., & Cocco, R. (2017). Effects in dogs with behavioural disorders of a commercial nutraceutical diet on stress and neuroendocrine parameters. *Veterinary Record, 180*(1), 18–18.

Chapter 8

1 Zahn, R., Moll, J., Paiva, M., Garrid, G., Krueger, F., Huey, E. D., & Grafman, J. (2009). The Neural Basis of Human Social Values: Evidence from Functional MRI, *Cerebral Cortex, 19*(2), 276–283, https://doi.org/10.1093/cercor/bhn080

2 Hecht, J., Miklósi, Á., & Gácsi, M. (2012). Behavioral assessment and owner perceptions of behaviors associated with guilt in dogs. *Applied Animal Behaviour Science, 139*(1–2), 134–142.

3 Horowitz, A. (2009). Disambiguating the 'guilty look': Salient prompts to a familiar dog behaviour. *Behavioural Processes, 81*(3), 447–452.

4 Brown, C. M., & McLean, J. L. (2015). Anthropomorphizing dogs: Projecting one's own personality and consequences for supporting animal rights. *Anthrozoös, 28*(1), 73–86.

5 Kogan, L. R., Bussolari, C., Currin-McCulloch, J., Packman, W., & Erdman, P. (2022). Disenfranchised guilt – Pet owners' burden. *Animals, 12*(13), 1690.

Chapter 9

1 Anderson, K. L., Casey, R. A., Cooper, B., Upjohn, M. M., & Christley, R. M. (2023). National dog survey: describing UK dog and ownership demographics. *Animals, 13*(6), 1072.

2 Sommerville, R., O'Connor, E. A., & Asher, L. (2017). Why do dogs play? Function and welfare implications of play in the domestic dog. *Applied Animal Behaviour Science, 197*, 1–8.

3 Rooney, N. J., Bradshaw, J. W., & Robinson, I. H. (2000). A comparison of dog–dog and dog–human play behaviour. *Applied Animal Behaviour Science, 66*(3), 235–248.

4 Rossi, A., Parada, F. J., Stewart, R., Barwell, C., Demas, G., & Allen, C. (2018). Hormonal correlates of exploratory and play-soliciting behavior in domestic dogs. *Frontiers in Psychology, 9*, 1559.

5 Romero, T., Nagasawa, M., Mogi, K., Hasegawa, T., & Kikusui, T. (2015). Intranasal administration of oxytocin promotes social play in domestic dogs. *Communicative & Integrative Biology, 8*(3), e1017157.

Index

overshadowing 34–5, 82
overweight dogs 93
owner preferences, canine 3–6
owner responses, canine attunement to
    52, 53–6, 57, 60, 62–5
oxytocin xiii, 13, 97–8, 179–80

Packer, Rowena 141–2
pain, and aggressive behaviour 133
'parenting' dogs 90–6, 164–6, 188
Pavlov, Ivan 26
pens 167
Pentagon terror attack, 2001 118
personality traits 90, 163–4
perspectives, human 90, 163, 164, 187
phenylacetic acid 12
phenylethylamine 12
pheromones 118
pitch 80–1
pituitary gland 36
place, and learning 31–2, 33, 40
play 172–3
    human playmate choice 176–8, 179,
        180, 185
    purpose of 175–81
    as reward 130
pointing 6, 79–81
police 37
post-traumatic stress disorder (PTSD)
    118
posterior superior temporal sulcus
    (pSTS) 58
postmen 47–8, 50, 55, 74
praise 10–11, 78
    as reward 15, 39
'predatory' behaviours 162
    see also prey drive
predictability 16–17, 110
preferences (canine)
    for people 3–6
    for rewards 11, 13, 38, 181
prefrontal cortex 9, 36, 112, 116, 158
prey drive xi, 41, 43–4
Prichard, Ashley 56
primates 79, 187
    see also chimpanzees
projection 163–4
proof-testing 123, 184
prosocial behaviour 13
protection dogs ix
protein 129, 136–8, 141, 143

high-protein diets 137
hydrolysed 134
low-protein diets 137, 138, 142, 144
punishment
    negative (withholding rewards) 82–3
    see also reprimands; scolding
puppies
    and allelomimetic behaviour 50–1
    and communication 80–1
    'puppy parties' 172–3, 175

quality of life 110
quality time 5–6, 190
'quiet' command 82–4

rats 98, 139
recall commands 23–45, 174
    calling your dog away from other dogs
        30, 42
    and disengagement training 183–5
    ignoring xiii, 30, 34–6, 39, 42, 174–5,
        178, 180, 183, 185, 188
    and punishments 43
    rock-solid 37–41
    vital nature of 41–2
rehomed dogs 24, 49–50, 162–3
reinforcement
    negative 119–22, 124–5
    positive 41, 70, 74, 83, 122, 123–4, 126
    see also self-reinforcing behaviours
reinforcers 11, 38
relaxation training 16–20, 100–2, 117–18
reprimands
    timely 169
    see also scolding
rescue dogs 102, 118–19
resilience 188
resource guarding 96, 102, 103–4
responses 63
reward system 8–11, 14, 55, 77–8, 94, 130
rewards 104, 189
and barking on command 81–2
    calorie value 182
    and conditioning 27, 28
    and the context shift effect 31
    and correct walking position 122
    and counter-conditioning 64–6
    and dog socialisation training 181–4
    and dopamine release 9
    food as 145–6, 181
    fuss as 73–4